THE HERITAGE INDUSTRY

Robert Hewison published his first book, *John Ruskin: The Argument of the Eye*, in 1976. He has written on the theatre for the *Sunday Times* since 1981. He is a recognised expert on the work of John Ruskin, but he has also examined the effects of censorship on the Monty Python team, and has written a history of the Cambridge Footlights. *The Heritage Industry* follows Hewison's series of books on 'The Arts in Britain since 1939', the first part of which – *Under Siege* – appeared in 1977, and which he has followed with two more titles – *In Anger* (1981) and *Too Much* (1986). This new book highlights the most significant feature of cultural life in present-day Britain . . . its obsession with the past.

Chris Orr follows in the tradition of Hogarth, Gillray and Rowlandson. He was born in Islington in 1943 and grew up in South London. He was a student at Ravensbourne, Hornsey and the Royal College of Art, where he is now a tutor in the printmaking department.

Besides being represented at international exhibitions, such as the Bradford Print Biennale (where he was a prize winner), the Ljubljana Print Biennale and the Norwegian Print Biennale, he has exhibited in Paris, New York, Tokyo and Stockholm, and has regular one-man shows at the Thumb Gallery in London. Chris Orr is married to the actress Catherine Terris and lives in Buckingham, where he has his print studio.

He has been a frequent visitor to Paddington station since the age of nine, when he was a train spotter.

Allan Titmuss's photographs – mostly of writers and musicians – appear regularly in newspapers and periodicals and on bookjackets and record sleeves both here and in the United States.

He lives in Surrey, 'with a refrigerator full of Kodak film, and never quite enough Nikon equipment'. His main recreation is crawling about in the dark at Ronnie Scott's Jazz Club.

In 1987 he was named Arts Photographer of the Year for his work with the *Observer*.

ROBERT HEWISON

THE HERITAGE INDUSTRY

Britain in a climate of decline

A Methuen Paperback

DRAWINGS BY CHRIS ORR

PHOTOGRAPHS BY ALLAN TITMUSS

by the same author

John Ruskin: The Argument of the Eye (Thames & Hudson)
Ruskin and Venice (Thames & Hudson)
New Approaches to Ruskin – editor (Routledge & Kegan Paul)
The Ruskin Art Collection at Oxford: The Rudimentary Series (Lion & Unicorn Press)
Under Siege: Literary Life in London 1939–45 (Weidenfeld & Nicolson)
In Anger: Culture in the Cold War 1945–60 (Weidenfeld & Nicolson)
Too Much: Art and Society in the Sixties 1960–75 (Methuen)
Irreverence, Scurrility, Profanity, Vilification and Licentious Abuse: Monty Python – The Case Against (Methuen)
Footlights: A Hundred Years of Cambridge Comedy (Methuen)

A METHUEN PAPERBACK
First published in Great Britain in 1987
by Methuen London Ltd
11 New Fetter Lane, London EC4P 4EE
Text copyright © Robert Hewison 1987
Drawings copyright © Chris Orr 1987
Photographs copyright © Allan Titmuss 1987

British Library Cataloguing in Publication Data

Hewison, Robert
   The heritage industry : Britain in a
   climate of decline.
   1. Great Britain—Civilization—20th
   century
   I. Title
   306′.0941   DA566.4

ISBN 0-413-16110-2

Printed and bound in Great Britain by
R. J. Acford Ltd, Chichester, Sussex

for
E.J.H.

CONTENTS

LIST OF PHOTOGRAPHS

INTRODUCTION

This book grew out of hearing it regularly asserted that every week or so, somewhere in Britain, a new museum opens. The statistic seemed so astonishing that it needed checking. When it turned out to be more or less accurate, it seemed appalling. How long would it be before the United Kingdom became one vast museum? And therein lies the paradox of this book: individually, museums are fine institutions, dedicated to the high values of preservation, education and truth; collectively, their growth in numbers points to the imaginative death of this country.

Most of the organisations which I criticise in this book have similarly worthy aims, but viewed together they present a picture of a country obsessed with its past, and unable to face its future. We like to think of our great cultural institutions as somehow neutral, mere facilities for the presentation of individual acts of creation, yet they profoundly affect our perception of what is judged to be history or art. As institutions they help to form the culture which they are assumed merely to reflect. A display in a museum may simply be telling a story, but the existence of a museum has a story to tell.

The story of this book is of the growth of a new cultural force of which museums are only a part. I call it the 'heritage industry' not only because it absorbs considerable public and private resources, but also because it is expected more and more to replace the real industry upon which this country's economy depends. Instead of manufacturing goods, we are manufacturing *heritage*, a commodity which nobody seems able to define, but which everybody is eager to sell, in particular those cultural institutions that can no longer rely on government funds as they did in the past. Which means every single one, from the universities to the Arts Council.

The reason for the growth of this new force is suggested by my subtitle: whatever the true figures for production and employment, this country is gripped by the perception that it is in decline. The heritage industry is an attempt to dispel this climate of decline by exploiting the economic potential of our culture, and it finds a ready market because the perception of decline includes all sorts of insecurities and doubts (which are more than simply economic) that makes its products especially attractive and reassuring. Looking at a Laura Ashley catalogue, it is possible that we imagine ourselves living in a museum already.

At best, the heritage industry only draws a screen between ourselves and our true past. I criticise the heritage industry not simply because so many of its products are fantasies of a world that never was; not simply because at a deeper level it involves the preservation, indeed reassertion, of social values that the democratic progress of the twentieth century seemed to be doing away with, but because, far from ameliorating the climate of decline, it is actually worsening it. If the only new thing we have to offer is an improved version of the past, then today can only be inferior to yesterday. Hypnotised by images of the past, we risk losing all capacity for creative change.

It may seem odd for a historian to criticise an obsession with history, though it is not so odd for a cultural historian to criticise the institutions upon which the maintenance of culture depends. My second chapter is intended to make clear a firm belief in the need for a past and for an understanding of history. Nostalgia, though a sickness that has reached fever point, can have an integrative effect by helping us to adjust to change. My appreciation of the fact that you don't know where you are unless you know where you have been is demonstrated by the amount of history there is in this book. But heritage is not history, and my worry is where we are going.

The growth of a heritage culture has led not only to a distortion of the past, but to a stifling of the culture of the present. Thus the narrative at the centre of the book moves forward from the origins of the conservation movement, through the post-war growth in museums of all kinds, but particularly industrial museums, to the present position of the Arts Council, an institution nominally concerned with the encouragement of contemporary culture, but more and more the victim of the economic and political pressures which stimulate the growth of the heritage industry.

I say economic and political pressures, but economics and politics are themselves culturally conditioned. We have a heritage politics as well as a heritage culture; their mutual influence on our economic situation is such that all three can be seen as the products of the same deep social convulsion caused by the twin disruptions of modernisation and recession since 1945. The urge to preserve as much as we can of the past is understandable, but in the end our current obsessions are entropic: that is to say, as the past solidifies around us, all creative energies are lost. Through entropy all things become equally inert; in thermodynamics it means the end of heat and light, form, matter and motion. In culture, entropy will leave us frozen in a dead moment of stopped time.

The answer to the problems which the heritage industry is exacerbating, rather than relieving, is, first of all, to realise what is going on. Once it is appreciated how many things there are to which the word 'heritage' is attached, from national institutions to garage doors, the word becomes absurd. My chief aim, then, is to describe the condition which afflicts us. The remedy I believe is the substitution of a critical, for a heritage culture.

Since, as I argue in my last chapter, even the radical wing of post-modernism betrays a deep, if parodic, obsession with the past, such a critical culture is only fragmentarily in being. The focus of this book, which is on the general culture rather than individual works of art, has caused me to neglect the work of contemporary artists almost as much as the cultural institutions I criticise. But while a historian can describe bad history, he cannot prescribe good art. Until conditions have changed sufficiently for a new art to emerge, all the cultural historian can do, like the poet, is warn.

While the analysis I offer here has not been presented before, I must acknowledge my debt to the writings and conversation of Patrick Wright, whose *On Living in an Old Country* (Verso, 1985) appeared just as I was exploring the idea of national nostalgia in *Too Much*, the conclusion to my triology on the arts in Britain since 1939. I look forward to his new book on the culture of decline. I also received a great deal of encouragement from my friend Chris Orr, and I am delighted that our discussions have developed into a collaboration in this book. He and Allan Titmuss have both enlarged the possibilities of my argument greatly.

Although they may not appreciate the use I have made of their help, I am most grateful to the countless press and information officers who have patiently answered my sometimes obscure, sometimes banal enquiries. The book would not have been completed on time without the hospitality of the Tyrone Guthrie Centre at Annaghmakerigg in Ireland; its director Bernard Loughlin has managed to achieve a combination of sociability and solitude in which creativity can flourish.

I should like to thank three different editors who have contributed, without knowing it, to the making of this book. The first is Rosemary Hart, who asked me to present a documentary on museums for Radio 4, 'A Future for the Past', which gave me a first opportunity to survey the museum world in this country. The second is Roger

Burgess of BBC Newcastle, who then enabled me to explore the concept of the industrial museum in a film, 'The Man Who Made Beamish', and with whom I have been conducting further investigations. The third is John Whitley, reviews editor of the *Sunday Times*, who has sent me all over the country to review plays, and in the process enabled me to see a great deal more of Britain than is caught in the bright lights of the West End.

The fourth, and most important editor, is Geoffrey Strachan, who commissioned this book and saw it through both the technical and creative difficulties produced by the telescoped production schedule we imposed upon ourselves. I thank him for his patience, and his commitment. Lastly, I want to thank my wife Erica, who has had to put up with all the pains of writing a book against the clock, without any of the rewards. She has been more than an editor, but rather a muse – even if it is a bit heritage to say so.

Fetter Lane, June 1987.

THE LIVING MUSEUM

HOME SWEET HOME

TEA

I
LIVING IN A MUSEUM

The first sound in the morning was the thumping of a British Rail InterCity rushing north to Blackpool, and the swish of tyres on wet tarmac. They don't wear clogs in Wigan any more, except at the Wigan Heritage Centre.

It is exactly fifty years since George Orwell published *The Road to Wigan Pier*, and his name still raises hackles in the town. He chose Wigan as the symbol of a civilization 'founded on coal', and went there to study the effects of the industrial recession of the 1930s on the lives of working-class people in the mining and manufacturing districts of the north. It was the 'wreck of a civilization'[1] and its victims were the people of Wigan, the products of the ugliness of industrialism. The couple Orwell found most repellent were 'the Brookers', who kept a tripe shop and lodging house where he stayed. Waking to the sound of the mill-girls' clogs on the cobbled street, he reflected on the narrow lives of the injured miner, the elderly surface worker, and the floating population of commercial travellers, newspaper-canvassers and hire-purchase touts with whom he shared the fetid room. He observed the habits of the unemployed derelict and the two old age pensioners who also lived in the Brookers' house. But his true horror was reserved for this complaining, self-pitying couple, she a gross invalid who lay on a sofa in the kitchen, he a resentful scrounger who was always dirty.

> But it is no use saying that people like the Brookers are just disgusting and trying to put them out of mind. For they exist in tens and hundreds of thousands; they are one of the characteristic by-products of the modern world. You cannot disregard them if you accept the civilization that produced them. For this is part at least of what industrialism has done for us. Columbus sailed the Atlantic, the first steam engines tottered into motion, the British squares stood firm under the French guns at Waterloo, the one-eyed scoundrels of the nineteenth century praised God and filled their pockets; and this is where it all led – to labyrinthine slums and dark back

15

kitchens with sickly, ageing people creeping round and round them like blackbeetles.[2]

Whatever Wigan thinks of Orwell, he wrote that he liked Wigan very much – the people, not the scenery – and that his one disappointment was that the Wigan Pier he had set his heart on seeing had been demolished. He did not know it but the original elevated tramway that is believed to be the source of the music hall joke with which George Formby Senior had made his home town famous, long before Orwell made it infamous, disappeared around 1910. Nor was it in the Wigan canal basin, but at Newton two miles away. But the myth stuck, and by the 1920s the name was attached, not to a pier in the seaside sense, but to a small iron frame used to tip up coal trucks to empty them into barges on the Liverpool–Leeds canal. There were several such tipplers along the canal, but the name was particularly associated with Bankes's Pier in the canal basin. The actual tippler disappeared in 1929, sold for £34 worth of scrap.

And then in 1984 it reappeared again. A group of students from Wigan College of Technology – no longer called the Mining and Technical College now that the mines had gone – reinstated the two metal rails curved up like tusks that had stood on the canal's edge. It was all part of a decision by the Labour-controlled Wigan Metropolitan Borough Council to turn its back on the industrial past, by restoring its features. The decaying nineteenth-century warehouses opposite the pier were refurbished, the site cleaned up, architected and planted, and re-opened as the Wigan Pier Heritage Centre.

At the heart of the site, which covers eight acres along either side of the canal, including a branch arm that leads to a fine stone warehouse, is the exhibition 'The Way We Were'. The Brookers do not feature. Instead, on the outside of the building is a sepia portrait photograph as big as an advertising hoarding, that shows a solid Wigan family, confronting the camera on the cobbles in front of their house. The father in Kitchener moustache wears a suit, stiff collar and tie, the mother wears shot silk, the daughter is in ringlets, the eldest boy in knickerbockers and an Eton collar, his younger siblings wear versions of sailors suits. A local graffiti artist has caused the hands of two of the boys to bleed with milky stigmata, and the wind has picked at the hoarding.

The family are inviting us to Wigan, 1900, a neat time shift that both avoids Orwell's 1930s, and places us at a moment when Wigan was doing well, 'a prosperous year, one of the few in this century not marked by economic depression or international struggle', as the tour guide has it.[3] £1.25 buys a ticket for a journey that does not begin in Wigan at all, but in an Ealing Comedy fantasy world of turn of the

century seaside piers, 'Happy Memories, Wakes Week 1900'. In this nostalgic holiday atmosphere you half expect the dummy in the railway signal box to be a young Alec Guinness, leaning down to another Alec Guinness dressed as 'the Card' in Arnold Bennett's novel. Only when you have strolled along the pier and turned the handles of the picture-card machines do you confront a notice, 'Back to Reality', and meet a cardboard diorama of Wigan station, black and lowering. The background tape of seagulls and pier-music gives way to hooters.

You enter Wigan through a coal mine, with more, sweating dummies, though the main passage is high enough for even the exceptionally tall George Orwell to stand up in. The economy and geography of Wigan are introduced to us: 'Wigan Was Built on Coal', but cotton was also King, and there is brass, pewter and a display of agricultural machinery from the Albion iron works. Dummies are hard at work in the nailmaking shop and the tinsmiths. Elsewhere sacks are eternally suspended in mid-heave, and farm workers stare for ever into the fire in the farmers' bar of the Park Hotel, reconstructed here after this 'perfect example of a Wigan pub' closed in 1985. Tussauds-like, an old man will never get off the lavatory in the backyard close.

Time is suspended – but it does not stand still. Outside the miner's cottage on the second floor one of the costumed figures has begun to move. It is Kitty, daughter of Harold Cooper, who lived there and whose imaginary body now lies screwed down in the coffin in the front room. Kitty opens the back door to her father's cottage, shrugs up her shawl, and in assumed Wigan accents asks if we have come to pay our respects. She brings us in, and explains that her father was crushed in a roof fall a month before, but died out of the pit, 'so there's no compensation'. The coffin is closed because he didn't look too good when he died. The gas mantle is burning above the coffin and the atmosphere is oppressive as she informs us that the funeral will be in the chapel in Scarisbrick Street. She invites us to share her grief and put a hand on the coffin as we file out. Implicated, even moved, we do so.

This is not the only performance at the Wigan Heritage Centre, for the brochure tells us to 'Above all, talk to the people of 1900'. A team of seven actors and a director are the first professional performers in Britain to be permanently employed in bringing such a display to life. Each researches a character and creates a scenario around one of the exhibits. The longest running performance is the schoolroom, where late twentieth-century children are subjected to a nineteenth-century lesson in arithmetic. 'Why should the weaver go deaf?' 'Why should the spinner go blind?' cries a young suffragette, standing on a cart otherwise occupied by immobile, plaster workers. Her feminist arguments are greeted with derisive cheers by anoraked visitors.

Had Orwell visited Wigan in 1976 rather than 1936, though much of the domestic squalor he described has been swept away, replaced by a squalor of a different order, the scenery of Wigan might well have appeared to him even uglier, and the possibilities of recovery more slight: by then thirty per cent of the area of Wigan was classified as derelict, more than in any other town in Britain. Between 1911 and 1970 the number of collieries fell from four hundred to eleven; 350 miles of railtrack lay abandoned, 1,100 textile mills had closed since 1951, the polluted canal carried no goods. In the 1980s the situation got even worse, with virtually no mining left, and the cotton trade gone forever. There were few service industries ready to replace coal or cotton, and by 1983 unemployment officially stood at 18.8 per cent, though on some of the housing estates it was as high as ninety per cent.

The houses around Wigan Pier had been demolished, replaced by a so-called industrial estate of small garages, garment factories, tyre centres, carpet warehouses and the inevitable DIY superstore. Most of the mills around the canal stood empty. In 1980 Courtaulds was preparing to close down its operation at the huge 1907 Trencherfield Mill nearby when the Borough Council persuaded them to stay, by buying the building and leasing back enough space to secure three hundred jobs. In 1982 British Waterways, who owned the warehouses opposite Wigan Pier, applied for planning permission to demolish the decaying buildings and redevelop the site. In 1973 Wigan Corporation had actually offered to pay British Waterways most of the cost of demolition of these 'unsightly premises', and had been refused.[4] But by 1982 a change of perception had taken place. The oldest structure, a stone warehouse built in 1777, though roofless and decayed, was now a Grade II listed building. Wigan, backed by Greater Manchester Council, decided to do something with its past. The past, after all, was virtually all it had left.

The key, as the report by the tourism consultant brought in by the Council succinctly argues, has been to be grateful to George Formby Senior, to Orwell and the Brookers. 'The name Wigan Pier is an inestimably valuable marketing asset, which should be exploited. To do so will turn the old joke round, and improve Wigan's image far more effectively than attempting to bury it would.' The consultant suggested exploiting not just the joke, but also the new-found popularity of the recent past, with the spread of theme parks, historic

19

enactments, industrial museums and interactive displays. The report stresses Wigan as 'a sadly typical example of decay and dereliction' and speculates that 'we may now be seeing the end of an era which began with the industrial revolution, and of the whole way of life, culture and traditions which sprang from it.' The problem was not just economic, but social.

> Traditions do not easily survive social change, at least among a new generation that has never experienced the circumstances that bred them. Since World War II, the improvements in living standards, the provision of unemployment and social service benefits, the growth of television and car ownership have greatly eroded the old ways of life. The disappearance of much of the industry which created the towns in the first place will accelerate the trend.[5]

'The Way We Were' would be an act of restoration of much more than a derelict canal basin.

The transformation has cost three and a half million pounds, and was achieved in such a short time that Her Majesty the Queen was able officially to open the centre in March 1986. Although the initiative was Wigan's, much of the money was not. As an assisted area Wigan qualifies for money from the European Economic Community under the Social Fund, to help job creation, and under the Regional Development Fund to assist tourism. Half a million pounds was raised that way. The English Tourist Board contributed £150,000. The Greater Manchester Council, in its dying days before abolition in 1986, was generous; money came from the Department of the Environment and the Countryside Commission, and there was help from the North West Museums and Galleries Service; Peter Walker Ltd.; British Telecom and the National Coal Board. Crucially, the Heritage Centre is a mixed development in partnership with private enterprise. The listed 1777 canal building was leased to a local property developer who rebuilt it stone by stone, and converted it into 7,500 square feet of offices with the help of a grant from the Department of the Environment. The Education Field Study Centre and the Pier Shop share premises with the Orwell pub, opened in 1984 in a warehouse refurbished by a brewery. Trencherfield Mill, which is included in the heritage site, houses not only Courtaulds but 'The Mill at the Pier', a concert and leisure centre, and the fashion department of Wigan Technical College, besides a machinery exhibition hall and the largest working mill steam engine in Britain – though its power is no longer applied to any purpose other than to awe spectators.

Essential as this economic interaction is to the project, it conditions what it is that people have ostensibly come to see. 'A heritage centre is not a museum,' states the consultant's report. 'The main point is to present a theme, not to display a collection of objects.'[6] There are other pointers: the first director, Peter Lewis, adopted the title 'piermaster', and his former career was not in the museum service, but commerce, and, significantly, marketing The Royal Exchange Theatre in Manchester. (Even more significantly, he has recently become the director of an institution that does call itself a museum, Beamish Open Air Museum, outside Newcastle.) Although the displays cannot avoid the realities of working life, even in a relatively prosperous 1900, they are studiously neutral when dealing with the responsibility for such conditions, or for catastrophes like the Maypole Pit Disaster of 1908, when seventy-six miners died.

Although the schools centre does function as an educational resource, the main purpose of Wigan Pier is to create, not so much an informative, as an emotional experience, a symbolic recovery of the way we were. The displays, recorded sounds and performances prompt recollections for the pensioners who seem to throng the centre; for younger people they present memories unexperienced, but ready formed. The buildings are not how they were – some were demolished as part of the restoration, including a small engineering works. A wooden canal walk has been built to provide access; the pier now faces a car park and a floating restaurant. The canalside has been landscaped, and a Bantam canal tug concreted into the shrubbery. We pass effortlessly from the bar of the Park Hotel in the Heritage Centre to the Orwell Pub, with its fake Tiffany lamps and genuine space invaders, from the 1900 grocer's store to the Pier Shop, where we can buy 'Mr Hunter's range of Victorian perfumes, soaps and medications', Wigan Pier Humbugs, Country Way Kiwi Fruit and Lemon Preserve, model miners' lamps, gourmet herb gardens, commemorative plates of the Royal opening bearing portraits of the Queen, and copies of *The Road to Wigan Pier*.

This anticipated expenditure is a clue to the theme of Wigan Pier. The past has been summoned to the rescue of the present; the three and a half million pounds has been invested in old buildings to stimulate an ageing economy. It is too soon to tell whether the injection has worked. Although attracting 300,000 visitors in its first year, three times the expected number, the Centre has not yet broken even on its running costs. Unemployment in the area is still above eighteen per cent, and much of Wigan looks battered and exhausted. Other buildings near the canal, now a conservation area, are empty or decayed. Swan Meadow Mills has been divided up into industrial units; a board outside shows thirteen out of seventeen are to let.

There is more space to let in the Wigan workshops, occupied by Swan Meadow Health Club, Impact Components and Photo-Me-Studios. The huge armature of machinery raised on a plinth in the Trencherfield Mill car park looks like a forlorn monument to a prehistoric age.

There are encouraging signs. Within sight of Wigan Pier, Northern Sailmakers Ltd have restored their warehouse and moved their headquarters to Wigan from Cheshire. Milliken, an American carpet manufacturing company has chosen Wigan for its European headquarters. The reclamation of derelict land has been sufficiently extensive for Pennington Flash – a lake created by mining subsidence – to become a 1,100-acre country park and bird-watching attraction. In the town centre, the drive which caused the council to refurbish the canal basin has caused it to demolish the fine Victorian market buildings, and construct 'the Galleries' in a £30 million partnership with local developers that will create new markets, seven large stores and seventy small shopping units, with parking for 700 cars. That is why the fittings of the Park Hotel that once served the farmers on market day have ended up in the Heritage Centre. The Galleries' only contact with the past will be the red brick facing and mock Tudor details in the balconies and eaves.

Development continues. In the Spring of 1987 a new café-bar opened in one of the semi-derelict alleys off Wallgate. It is called the Officers' Club. Although a man in a dinner-jacket stands at the door to repel undesirables, it is not a club; there are no officers, nor are there likely to be. It is 'an exciting new concept' belonging to the owners of the Pier Disco, an externally shabby warehouse in the canal basin. Here the future and the past collide: the bar boasts a satellite TV monitor 'enabling the businessman to keep ahead of world financial news as it happens' but more likely to watch 'the cricket from Australia or the yachting from America.'[7] In the bar upstairs there is £10,000 worth of solid glass grand piano, imported from Japan.

These high-tech features are framed in a confusing décor collaged from *The World of Interiors*. City sophisticated art-deco lights stand uncomfortably with bamboo and glass tables, palm trees and Raffles Hotel overhead fans. Pompadour colours of green and gold flow from the walls, that appear to be ragged, but may well be papered. The 'conservatory' has ruched curtains which cannot rise or fall, there are panels of brand new leaded stained glass below the level of the ceiling. Wicker arm chairs (country house conservatory) sit round cast-iron and marble topped tables (Edwardian sawdust and spittoon). And on the walls are the old photographs, the unlabelled views and anonymous family groups of an ersatz past, silently staring into a space filled by the backbeat of homogenized American rock. The Brookers

are not here either, and the man at the door would keep them out.

Wigan Borough Council is spending £200,000 a year to promote the economy that has produced the Officers' Club. A council brochure that frames the tower of Trencherfield Mill in a freshly painted arch of Wigan Pier tells us simply 'Forget the traditional myths' and then extols 'The Way We Were'. At the Officers' Club a former piano salesman who had been out of work for five years after the factory closed down, sits at his Japanese piano, and plays 'As Time Goes By'.

Wigan is not an isolated example, any more than it was in 1936. There are now at least forty-one Heritage Centres in Britain. While future perspectives seem to shrink, the past is steadily growing. The increase in the number of museums in Britain has been such that until recently no one could say how many there were. It is still difficult to be precise. The Museums Association published the most accurate survey in 1987: having started with 3,537 institutions that might qualify, these were reduced to 2,131, of which 1,750 replied to the association's questionnaire.[8] Of these, half have been founded since 1971. The Director of the Science Museum, Dr Neil Cossons, has said 'You can't project that sort of rate of growth much further before the whole country becomes one big open air museum, and you just join it as you get off at Heathrow.'[9]

The urge to protect and preserve the past extends to the whole of the built and natural environment. Living in an old country, we have plenty to protect. The Royal Commission on Historical Monuments was set up in 1908 to make 'an inventory of the Ancient and Historical monuments and constructions connected with or illustrative of the contemporary culture, civilization and conditions of life of the people of England' – and nearly seventy years later still has not finished its work.[10] Since the principle of listing buildings in order to inhibit their demolition or alteration was first introduced in 1947 the number has steadily grown, and is expected to reach half a million in 1988, double the number in 1982. But the latest changes to the system mean that the potential number is infinite. The cut-off date will no longer be 1939, but a rolling period by which any building more than thirty years old may qualify for protection. In addition to individually protected buildings there are at least 5,558 conservation areas and some 200 town schemes which impose planning controls.

In 1980 there were 45,000 licensed places of worship in England and Wales; if Scotland and Northern Ireland are added, the total is between 60,000 and 70,000. The Church of England has 16,643 churches, of which 8,500 are pre-Reformation: in all, including

cathedrals, 12,013 are listed buildings. The Redundant Chu
Fund looks after 200. The government, through the Property Se
Agency, is responsible for more than a thousand listed building:

The principle of scheduling ancient monuments is older thai
of listing occupied buildings. When the first Ancient Monument
was passed in 1882, the schedule attached to it identified just :
eight sites. The number has now reached 12,800, and that is o
fraction of the 635,000 sites that could be considered. The Anᴄᴵᴇnt
Monument and Archeological Areas Act of 1979 has extended archaeological protection by allowing the designation of an 'area of archeological importance' where archeological studies must be carried out
before development takes place. So far five have been declared, in
Canterbury, York, Chester, Exeter and Hereford.

The countryside receives protection through the ten National Parks
administered by the Countryside Commission, the extensive holdings
of the National Trust, the declaration of areas of Special Scientific
Interest, nature reserves and the work of the Nature Conservancy
Council, the Royal Society for the Protection of Birds, and the
lobbying of the Council for the Protection of Rural England and
Friends of the Earth.

The principal government agency involved in protecting and
enlarging this inheritance of land and buildings is the Department of
the Environment, formed in 1970 to reconcile the conflicting interests
of the former Ministries of Housing and Local Government, Public
Building and Works, Transport and Planning. The Department's
Directorate of Ancient Monuments and Historic Buildings maintains
the Royal Parks, and the occupied and unoccupied royal palaces. It is
responsible for listing buildings and scheduling monuments, and
sponsors the Countryside Commission together with five 'heritage'
agencies: The Historic Buildings and Monuments Commission, the
Royal Commission on Historical Monuments, the National Heritage
Memorial Fund, the Redundant Churches Fund and the Royal
Armouries.

The estimated expenditure of the Department of the Environment
on the built heritage in 1986/87 was £96 million. More than half of
this goes to the Historic Buildings and Monuments Commission,
which has adopted the name English Heritage. English Heritage
manages some 400 monuments and buildings, makes grants to
individuals and organisations to assist with historic buildings, conservation areas, town schemes, ancient monuments and rescue archeology. It advises on the listing of buildings and scheduling of
monuments, and on applications to demolish or alter such structures.
It is also expected to promote the appreciation of such places.

The Department of the Environment however is by no means the only government agency involved in heritage affairs. The Office of Arts and Libraries is the principal ministry concerned with museums and art galleries, and makes an equal contribution with the Department of the Environment to the National Heritage Memorial Fund. The Department of Employment sponsors the English Tourist Board which, under the Development of Tourism Act of 1969, receives some £9 million a year to invest in heritage projects. In this period of high unemployment the Manpower Services Commission is a significant supplier of labour, and the European Economic Community is also a source of funds. Nor should the role of local authorities be neglected. In 1985/86 the English authorities were estimated to be spending £44.9 million on environment enhancement and conservation.

The state's responsibility for conservation and the heritage, either through ministries or the quangos (Quasi-Autonomous Non-Government Organisations) that they fund, is closely interwoven with the work of independent voluntary organisations, some of which, like the National Trust, have their position recognised by Acts of Parliament. Usually the state has been the second, not the first on the scene, and the spread of the conservation movement can be followed through the chronology of the foundation of key voluntary bodies: the Commons, Footpaths and Open Spaces Preservation Society, 1865; the Society for the Protection of Ancient Buildings, 1877; the National Trust, 1895; the Ancient Monuments Society, 1921; the Council for the Care of Churches, 1922; the Council for the Protection of Rural England, 1926; the National Trust for Scotland, 1931; the Georgian Group 1937; the Vernacular Architecture Group, 1952; the Civic Trust, 1957; the Victorian Society, 1958; the Landmark Trust, 1963; the Thirties Society, 1979; the National Piers Society, 1980; the Railway Heritage Trust, 1985; the Historic Farm Buildings Trust, 1985; the Fountain Society, 1985. Not only has the pace of the conservation movement quickened, the objects of its concern have come closer and closer to the present day. How long will it be before a Fifties Foundation and a Sixties Society join the list?

The most important organisations meet every two months in the Joint Committee of the National Amenity Societies, made up of the Ancient Monuments Society, the Civic Trust, the Council for British Archeology, the Council for the Protection of Rural England, the Georgian Group, the National Trust, the National Trust for Scotland, the Society of the Protection of Ancient Buildings and the Victorian Society. The Victorian Society, SPAB, Georgian Group, Ancient Monuments Society and the Council for British Archeology are all involved in the statutory planning process, in that they have to be notified about applications to alter or demolish ancient buildings, and each receives £10,000 a year from the government for carrying out these functions.

Most prominent are the National Trust which, after the state, is the largest landowner in the United Kingdom, and the Civic Trust. The Civic Trust does not own land or buildings, but exercises its function of conserving and improving the environent both in town and country through its cooperation with local amenity societies. In 1957 when the Civic Trust was founded there were some 200 such societies, now there are nearly a thousand, with a combined estimated membership of 300,000 people. The Civic Trust also administers the Architectural Heritage Fund, set up in 1975, which is a major source of capital for conservation projects: £4½ million has been lent to 109 schemes by March 1986. The Landmark Trust preserves some 106 small buildings, and wherever possible puts them to use by letting them out as holiday homes. In all there are seventy-nine local building preservation trusts in England. There are at least 158 local archeological societies affiliated to the Council for British Archeology. In 1980 the Countryside Commission set up the Groundwork Scheme to clean up derelict industrial areas, leading to the foundation of six Groundwork Trusts which operate in cooperation with local authorities, the Nature Conservancy Council and the British Trust for Conservation Volunteers. The Crafts Council and the Council for Small Industries in Rural Areas help with the conservation of appropriate buildings.

These organisations, and the places for which they care, attract an ever growing public. It is estimated that 213 million sight-seeing visits were made in Britain in 1985, sixty-seven million of them to historic buildings. According to the 1986 edition of *Facts About the Arts* in 1983/84 the audience for the live arts of thirty-nine million was outnumbered both by the audience for historic houses, at forty-eight million, and museums and galleries at fifty-eight million – more even than the cinema at fifty-three million.[11] In 1986 there were at least 1,724 historic buildings and ancient monuments (excluding churches) open to the public, plus well over 200 historic houses open by appointment. Of the 1,724, forty-five per cent are privately owned, twenty-three per cent owned by local authorities, twenty-one per cent belong to the government or its agencies, eleven per cent belong to the National Trust. As many as forty per cent do not charge for admission, yet overall revenue has risen by thirty per cent since 1979, at constant prices. In Britain as a whole it is estimated that £110 million was spent by visitors to historic buildings and gardens. About a third of these visitors were foreign tourists, sixty-seven per cent of whom in 1984/85 visited historic sites, houses or cathedrals. The total earnings from overseas visitors to Britain in 1985/86 was £5,473 million.

★ ★ ★

The past, then, is a major economic enterprise. But then so is the atomic bomb. Activities do not justify themselves purely on the grounds that they contribute to the gross national product, otherwise we would have Councils for the Preservation of Prostitution and Crime. As Wigan Pier's consultant recognised, the conservation movement, as producer and consumer, answers a profound cultural need: it is this that makes the past such a tourist attraction.

The nostalgic impulse which constitutes such an important part of the conservationist frame of mind was a national cultural characteristic long before the Gothic Revival laid the foundations for the modern conservation movement. Both classicism and medievalism contain elements of nostalgia, in that they look back to imagined earlier aesthetics and states of mind. But their use of the past was somewhat different, in that they sought to re-use ancient elements in a creative way. The nostalgic impulse has waxed and waned, but is presently getting stronger, and twentieth-century nostalgia is of a new kind. Orwell was not free of it. Beside the Brookers we should set his recollections of 'the peculiar easy completeness, the perfect symmetry as it were, of a working-class interior at its best. Especially in winter evenings after tea, when the fire glows in the open range and dances mirrored in the steel fender, when Father, in shirt-sleeves, sits in the rocking chair at one side of the fire reading the racing finals, and Mother sits on the other with her sewing, and the children are happy with a penn'orth of mint humbugs. . . .' It is an image worthy of the Wigan Pier Heritage Centre, and the humbugs can be bought from the Pier Shop, but, Orwell adds sadly, 'This scene is still reduplicated in a majority of English homes, though not in so many as before the war.'[12]

The war in question is the First World War. Since the Second World War, nostalgia has become a dominant characteristic. Peter Conrad has given some concrete examples.

> Britten came home from America to the 'familiar streets' of East Anglia, and made music from his longing for social membership and acceptance in *Peter Grimes*. . . . Betjeman began his encylopaedic digressions to country churches and railway sidings. John Piper painted derelict nonconformist chapels as luminous with spirit as the Brideshead chapel, where a flame kindled by crusaders still burned. The photographer Bill Brandt studied the culture's buried past in the graveyards and vacant houses of his compilation *Literary Britain*. Though the Festival of Britain confected its architecture from atomic orbitals and left as its memento a Festival Hall which looks like a cumbrous television set, the earnest hope of the Fifties was that the future would bring

back the past. The coronation was supposed to inaugurate a second Elizabethan age. England had begun a re-perusal of its history, which continues yet.[13]

John Betjeman has been the most popular English poet of the latter half of the twentieth century, partly by dint of a second career as a television pundit extolling the virtues of Victorian villas and Edwardian suburbia. He is followed by Philip Larkin, a great admirer of Betjeman and a more serious poet; conservative and nostalgic – with a touch of bitterness at his impotence against change. Britain's most popular novelist, the most read writer in our public libraries is the historical and romantic novelist Catherine Cookson. In the 1950s the first stirrings of the cult of youth was paradoxically signalled by London toughs dressing in Edwardian clothes; even the 1960s, when there was a rare moment of confidence and expansion, there was a strong vein of nostalgia. The Beatles were happiest as Sergeant Pepper's Lonely Hearts Club Band. Now, instead of the young meteors of the Sixties, today's heroes are young fogies, their fashionable pre-eminence contested only by the New Georgians, a middle-class cult with none of the menace of the Teds.

The look back in nostalgia has become an economic enterprise, as the commercial interests of manufacturers and advertising have recognised. This nostalgia is in part one for a lost sense of authenticity, a nostalgia that consumes ploughman's lunches and campaigns for real ale. Commerce reinforces the longing for authenticity in order to exploit it. As Peter Conrad has written

> Virtually everything we consume is touted as a magic potion, capable of transporting us back to a pastoral infancy before our taste-buds sickened and before the country slumped into modernity. Hovis has turned the baking and breaking of bread into a sacrament. In its commercials, gnarled elders toil at a feudal mill or trudge through a countryside sentimentally soothed by a mist of retrospection. The Hovis company's mystique is northern – tough, gritty, grainy – but it derives its mythology from the south-west, with advertisements filmed in Hardy country.[14]

Commerce, which is no fool and employs market researchers, recognises that nostalgia is also deeply linked with snobbery, beginning with the careful marketing of the Royal Family both as cosy, domestic paradigms, and symbols of fairy-tale splendour. The Royal Family are at the heart of the English season, that display of heritage events from Ascot to the shooting season which, in 1987, appears to have been sponsored by Veuve Clicquot. 'One elegant definition of the English season might be all those events at which the great champagne house of Veuve Clicquot is on sale,' writes Godfrey Smith in his introduction to *The English Season* (£14.95) which Veuve Clicquot have helped to publish.[15] The Mountbatten family has gone into marketing, by licensing Marketing Associates International to produce a range of luxury goods, such as dinner plates with the Mountbatten crest and reproductions of Lord Palmerston's desk, and a cookery book with 'traditional family recipes'.[16] The appetite for association with the rich and famous is fed by publications like *The Englishman's Room* and *The English Dog at Home*, where the dogs of the Queen, the Queen Mother, Princess Anne, two duchesses, a Lord, baronets and millionaires are depicted in their stately homes.[17]

Authenticity and snobbery, however, are only resonant elements of an all-embracing passion for the present past. The past is growing around us like ivy. The fashion writer Sarah Mower noted in January 1987

> The signs of creeping retroism are everywhere: in the success of Hackett's reconditioned vintage clothing for men, in the nostalgic mood of designer collections for women. For the past eighteen months we've had Edwardian riding habits and safari costumes that could have come out of a colonial lady's trunk. We've seen the revival of the bustle; the crinoline and the whaleboned corset are imminent for spring.[18]

One of the most successful publications of recent years has been *The Country Diary of an Edwardian Lady*, a title which manages to roll all the pastoralism, snobbery and retromania of nostalgia into one ball.[19] The *Country Diary* has sold over 2.6 million copies in thirteen languages, and has spawned not only *The Country Diary Book of Crafts* and *The Country Diary Book of Knitting*, but seventy-five million pounds' worth of merchandising, including Country Lady cosmetics.

The drive to conceal the present under layers of the past leads to the marketing of 1985 bottles of wine as 'The Turner Collection', the labels bearing the painter's signature and reproductions of 'The Fighting Téméraire Tugged to her Last Berth to be Broken Up' and 'Peace, Burial at Sea'. The 1986 Ideal Home Exhibition displayed a series of houses 'in a variety of period styles, from Tudor to the year 2000', thus reducing even the future to a period style. For the show the builders Potton erected 'a brand new model from their Heritage range' which 'whilst incorporating all the advantages of up to date standards and materials, still manages to generate that old world cottage atmosphere.' At the rear of the house bloomed the specially bred Potton Heritage rose.[20] A company in Watford can, without any trace of irony, sell the share certificates of bankrupt British companies as 'Heritage Originals'.

The actors of Wigan Pier demonstrate that we not merely wish to recall the past, buy souvenirs of the past or build and decorate our homes in past styles: we actually want to live in the past. Members of the Sealed Knot campaign the length and breadth of England in Royalist and Parliamentarian uniforms, but there are also Roman legionaries, Norman knights, medieval jousters, veterans of the Napoleonic War and of World War II – though the latter are required by law to wear either American or German uniforms. The Young National Trust Theatre was founded in 1976 as an educational aid, but 'the theatre gives much needed exposure to the nine Trust properties it visits each season. It is seen as a good marketing asset for the venues, and the tourist aspect is developed by encouraging visitors of all ages to participate.'[21] The logic of *The Country Diary of an Edwardian Lady* is being applied by an American heritage entrepreneur at Williamson Park, Lancaster, with a theme park offering us an Edwardian day out.

As the past begins to loom above the present and darken the paths to the future, one word in particular suggests an image around which other ideas of the past cluster: the heritage. The word has parliamentary approval in the National Heritage Acts of 1980 and 1983, which created the National Heritage Memorial Fund and English Heritage respectively. These should not be confused with National Heritage, the title adopted by the Museums Action Group in 1971, nor must we muddle Heritage in Danger, 1974, with SAVE Britain's Heritage, 1975. There is an All-Parliamentary Committee for the Heritage, a Society for the Interpretation of Britain's Heritage, a Heritage Education Trust and a Heritage Co-Ordination Group. Heritage centres and Heritage trusts multiply, and there is a World Heritage Convention.

Two things are clear about this word: it is a relatively recent usage – an important date was the designation of 1975 as European Architectural Heritage Year – and it is a word without definition, even in two Acts of Parliament. In the United States it has been appropriated by the New Right. The Heritage Foundation set up in 1973 has a twelve-million-dollar budget to fund a Washington think-tank that serves to promote conservative political philosophy on an international scale. It has had significant influence on the Reagan administration and its ideas have been favourably received by Mrs Thatcher and Chancellor

Kohl of West Germany. It helped to establish the Institute for European Defence and Strategic Studies in London in 1979, and it is credited with the decision of both the United States and Britain to withdraw from UNESCO. Quite separately, Heritage USA, a 2,300-acre inspirational theme park in Carolina, the third most popular tourist attraction in the United States after the Disneylands in Florida and California, is the centre of the Praise the Lord fundamentalist Christian television network.

In Britain, the use of the term is more diffuse. The keeper of the People's Palace in Glasgow describes the museum as the centre of the city's 'radical heritage'.[22] Patrick Cormack the Conservative MP who founded the All-Parliamentary Committee for the Heritage, and is now chairman of the Heritage Co-Ordination Group, has written

> When I am asked to define our heritage I do not think in
> dictionary terms, but instead reflect on certain sights and
> sounds. I think of a morning mist on the Tweed at Dryburgh
> where the magic of Turner and the romance of Scott both
> come fleetingly to life; of a celebration of Eucharist in a quiet
> Norfolk church, with the medieval glass filtering the colours,
> and the early noise of the harvesting coming through the
> open door; or of standing at any time before the Wilton
> Diptych. Each scene recalls aspects of an indivisible heritage
> and is part of the fabric and expression of our civilization.[23]

This pastoral, romantic and religiose evocation, not far from a Hovis commercial, in fact defines a very specific view of the heritage – but we can expect quite different sights and sounds at the Beamish Open Air Museum's annual Geordie's Heritage Day.

As Lord Charteris, the Chairman of the National Heritage Memorial Fund, and former private secretary to the Queen, has said, the heritage means 'anything you want'.[24] It means everything and it means nothing, and yet it has developed into a whole industry. At times, like Wigan Metropolitan Borough Council, we may feel that it is the only industry we have got.

THE CLIMATE OF DECLINE

George Orwell is part of the heritage now, his reputation safely
pinned by a plaque to the wall of a house in Islington. His
grimmest prophecies have been duly celebrated for not coming
to pass in 1984; his politics have been consigned to 'before the war'.
1937 is half a century away, and if we think of the period at all we are
more likely to conjure up an ambience than historical events: the
Thirties of Agatha Christie series on television, or the advertisements
for the Orient Express. Indeed, we can re-enter the world of Hercule
Poirot by taking the train, though it only goes as far as Venice, that
classic symbol of sinking European civilization.

The phrase 'before the war' needs no explanation as to which war
is meant. For Britain the period 1939–45 caused a break with the
past more thorough than 1914–18. Our imperial economic position
was so weakened that the conversion from Empire to Commonwealth
began with independence for India in 1947; domestically the war
forced social and political changes that led to the creation of the
Welfare State. 'After the war', the 1945 election seemed to be saying,
nothing was going to be the same.

Change is felt in many ways, but it is visibly expressed in the built
environment, where gradual alteration to the physical patterns of
everyday life register the consequences of social change. The war
meant that nearly all our cities experienced violent change: one third
of the City of London was destroyed by bombing, and ports and
manufacturing towns alike were damaged. Less obvious targets like
Bath, Exeter and Canterbury were attacked as cultural symbols. The
buildings that survived had received the minimum maintenance for
six years.

The post-war period began with an emphasis – within the limits of
necessary austerity measures – on reconstruction, and since some
700,000 homes had been destroyed during the war, on the building
of new houses. The Conservative government which took over from
Labour in 1951 outdid its predecessor in figures for new housing:
300,000 a year in the early 1950s. Both political parties wanted not
just new houses, but whole new towns. Twelve were designated by

35

1950, and a further ten between 1961 and 1970. In addition, planning policies continued to encourage the movement of people away from centres of big cities, over prophylactic green belts into some fifty expanded and overspill towns. By 1982 two million people were living in urban communities that had not existed in 1945.

The result of these policies was not quite the brave new world that the drafters of the Town and Country Planning Act of 1947 had intended. In 1955 the *Architectural Review* published Ian Nairn's polemical *Outrage*, a pictorial survey of environmental attrition framed by a photograph of 'rural England . . . a reminder of what we are squandering with all the means at our disposal, confident that there will always be some left over.' *Outrage* added a new word to the language: Subtopia.

> Within towns the agents of Subtopia are demolition and decay, buildings replaced by bijou gardens, car-parks and underscale structures, reduction of density where it should be increased, reduction of vitality by false genteelism, of which Municipal Rustic is the prime agent, the transporter of Subtopian blight to town and country alike, as is the badly detailed arterial road.[1]

Although the feelings expressed in *Outrage* had a practical outcome in the foundation of the Civic Trust in 1957, *Landscape in Distress*, a survey of 250 square miles of Oxfordshire carried out in 1965 demonstrated how mile by mile each small mistake – wirescape, infill, power line, road widening and unsympathetic private and public development continued to erode the environment.[2]

Outrage protested that while the planning offensive was started in a mood of idealism, the policy of dispersal was spreading Subtopia, not checking it. But already a new factor was at work that was about to bring an even more devastating change. In 1954 the requirement for building licences, which had restricted most commercial building to the reconstruction of war-damaged offices and factories, was abandoned. In London the Victorian regulation that limited the height of new buildings to eighty feet was lifted. The age of the high-rise had begun. In the next ten years an unprecedented building boom completely altered the scale and skylines of Britain's major cities. In London New Zealand House, the Shell Building, Millbank Tower, the Hilton Hotel, Campden Tower Notting Hill Gate, St Paul's Precinct, the London Wall development and the Royal Garden Hotel were all in place by 1964, when the new Labour government banned further office building. In 1963 the first property developer had been knighted.

The new architecture altered the symbolically 'national' environment of the capital (and since Labour's ban did not affect projects already started, construction continued until the Conservatives lifted it again in 1970), but every major local authority in the country saw the advantage to itself in profitable partnership with property developers. Their traffic planners wanted to accommodate the ever-increasing number of motor cars, their treasurers wanted to increase the rateable value of the properties they taxed. Through their powers to declare comprehensive redevelopment areas they were able to carry out wholesale demolition that wiped out old street patterns and neighbourhoods at the rate of eighty thousand houses a year. Much of this was called 'slum clearance' (no compliment to the people who lived there) but many sound houses went as well.

As new towns and 'overspill' were expensive and for a time less fashionable, the logic of the commercial skyscraper was applied to homes. By 1965 there were some 27,000 flats in new buildings over ten storeys high, 6,500 in blocks of twenty storeys or more. From the alienated heights of these structures people looked down on the empty wastes where their former homes had been, and turned back to watch *Coronation Street* on the television. The architect James Stirling said recently, 'The housing architecture of the 1960s was simply a matter of building more and more houses for less and less money until you ended up with a sort of trash.'[3] The new systems-building for the blocks of flats produced damp and decay, and, in the case of the collapse of part of Ronan Point in 1968, death. The memorial to the modernising of public housing in the 1960s was written by an anonymous resident in an overspill estate in Kirkby on Merseyside, when he told the Archbishop of Canterbury's Commission on Urban Priority Areas: 'People here have to live in a mistake.'[4]

The redevelopment of London began a fresh phase with the return of a Conservative government in 1970. In 1975, in *The Rape of Britain*, Colin Amery and Dan Cruickshank examined the damage done to thirty British towns and concluded: 'The destruction during the nineteenth century pales into insignificance alongside the licensed vandalism of the years 1950–75.'[5] In spite of legislation to protect buildings of historical significance and architectural merit, Department of the Environent statistics showed that listed buildings were being lost at the rate of one a day. 8,000 listed buildings were destroyed between 1957 and 1977. Road schemes deadened and blighted whole areas of towns and cities. The Ancient Monuments Society has estimated that a third of all applications to demolish listed buildings came from local authorities, with some of the largest applications in connection with road proposals.

Whatever the gains there were in new houses, new schools and amenities, the clearances, demolitions and dispersal also produced loss, a loss of a sense of location and identity, as the sociologists began to notice. Marc Fried wrote of the former inhabitants of an American urban renewal scheme in Boston

> For the majority it seems quite precise to speak of their reactions as expressions of *grief*. These are manifest in the feelings of painful loss, the continued longing, the general depressive tone, frequent symptoms of psychological or social or somatic distress, the active work required in adapting to the altered situation, the sense of helplessness, the occasional expressions of both direct and displaced anger, and the tendencies to idealise the lost place.[6]

While the urban environment of Britain became increasingly degraded and unfamiliar, the countryside suffered steady pressure from modernisation. Motorways, airports, power stations and overhead transmission lines, mineral workings, reservoirs, gas holders and natural gas terminals, besides new towns and housing estates, changed the landscape. The first few miles of motorway opened in 1958; by 1974 motorways had consumed 25,000 acres of agricultural land.

The modernisation of the railway system meant that following the Beeching Report of 1963 the number of passenger stations in use fell from 7,626 in 1949 to 2,364 in 1979, freight stations from 1,688 to 473.[7] The whole architectural environment of the rail network – signal boxes, water towers, sheds and wayside halts – was radically altered, leaving over 3,000 miles of abandoned railway line. Romantic steam gave way to mundane diesel. In 1982 there were more than 20,000 acres of derelict railway land.

In both town and country, modernisation seemed to produce dereliction. 175,000 acres of land in England, Scotland and Wales were officially recognised as derelict in 1974, to which must be added other waste and 'operational' land, producing a figure of nearly 500,000 ruined, abandoned or blighted acres. Yet, even greater changes were taking place in the land reserved for agriculture. 'Britain's world-famous town and country planning system is widely considered the most sophisticated and effective mechanism in the world for curbing the inherent tendency of powerful private interests to override public interest in land', wrote Marion Shoard in *The Theft of the Countryside*. 'So what,' she asks, 'has it been doing to safeguard our landscape heritage from the systematic onslaught launched by modern agriculture on the English landscape?'[8]

Her answer is 'almost nothing'. Farming and commercial forestry are 'effectively above the law as it applies to other activities which affect the environment'.[9] Between 1947 and 1980 half the woods that had existed in England before 1600 were felled. In the 1970s Dutch elm disease killed eleven million trees, while farmers bulldozed small woods and cleared away single trees. In 1979 the Nature Conservancy Council warned that broadleaf woods might not survive at all outside nature reserves. New planting largely consisted of regimented belts of conifers. In an effort to maximise the efficiency of new farm machinery (which was also contributing to the decline of the rural population) fields were enlarged and familiar patterns destroyed. Between 1946 and 1975 a quarter of the hedgerows in England and Wales – 120,000 miles – were grubbed up. Roughlands were ploughed, wetlands drained, so that only just over a quarter of the lowland heaths of the nineteenth century survive. Downs, moors and clifftops disappeared beneath uniform ryegrass or plantations of fir.

The man-made features of the ancient landscape, barrows, hill forts and archeological sites were eroded or destroyed altogether by deep ploughing. Mechanisation made old farm buildings obsolete, the amalgamation of farms into larger units caused whole groups to be abandoned. The process of change was accelerated by the Farm Capital Grants scheme operated by the Ministry of Agriculture from 1973. While the old buildings decayed, new factory-like structures rose beside them. In a survey carried out in 1977 an American architect found that out of sixty-six references to tithe barns, seven had been destroyed, eight could not be found, and of the forty-two survivors, a third were in a very bad state of repair.[10] Pre-war rural patterns crumbled in the face of the ecological asset stripping of the agri-business, surviving only in remote regions, or television's *All Creatures Great and Small*.

The effect of modernisation was not just that everything had changed, but that everything had become more and more the same, as architectural and scenic differences were ironed out under the weight of mediocrity and uniformity. In *The Coming of Post-Industrial Society* Daniel Bell argues that technology may have brought more substantial change to individual lives in the late nineteenth and early twentieth centuries, in the shape of railways, electricity, motor cars and aviation, but the post-war development of television and computers has imposed a tighter and more uniform social network. As Marshall McLuhan has also argued, the revolutions in transport and communication have created more interdependence and therefore less isolation. 'But along with a greater degree of interdependence has come a change of scale – the spread of cities, the growth of organisational

size, the widening of the political arena – which has made individuals feel more helpless within larger entities, and which has broadened the span of control over the activities of any organisation from a centre.'[11]

In Britain until the late 1960s material change was generally regarded as the price of progress that brought full employment after the depression of the 1930s. Rising affluence compensated for loss of international status. The decade was a period of intense social as well economic change, as new views were taken of the responsibilities of the individual and the role of the family: the Suicide Act 1961, the abolition of the death penalty in 1965, the legalisation of abortion in 1967, the Sexual Offences Act in that same year, and the Divorce Act in 1969. Censorship was relaxed by the Obscene Publications Act of 1959 and the Theatres Act of 1968. By 1969 the contraceptive pill was widely available on the National Health, with lasting consequences for attitudes to sexual morality. Since 1969 the weakening hold of traditional beliefs and the shifts of population have been reflected by the redundancy of 1053 churches.

The social revolution of the 1960s was perceived as the emergence of a new, permissive society. Its limits were defined in the 1970s, when a political reaction set in, but in spite of his sociological scepticism, Christie Davies concluded in his study that since the start of the Sixties 'people are more likely to indulge in normal and perverse sexual activities, to take drugs of varying degrees of addictiveness and to attack their fellow citizens either in order to rob them or just for the sheer pleasure of it.' But he also concluded that the loosening of traditional restraints in the Sixties seemed to have come about for no good reason. 'We have gained in tolerance, in compassion and in freedom, but not because of our belief in these values. We are tolerant not as a matter of principle but as an expression of moral indifference.'[12]

Christie Davies's pessimism reflects the increasing disillusion of the 1970s. Whereas the economic, social and environmental change of the first post-war period took place in an atmosphere of renewal and modernisation, subsequent change has taken place in a climate of decline.

The watershed between these two kinds of change, which have served to disconnect the immediate present from the perceived past, was the devaluation of the currency in 1967, at the beginning of a period of rapidly rising inflation and increasing unemployment. Emblematically, the coinage, whose traditional forms went back to the Roman introduction of *l.s.d.* was decimalised in 1970, a process which both disconnected the means of exchange from the past, and, it seems, further devalued 'the pound in your pocket' by stimulating inflation. The oil crisis of 1973 was a major economic blow, and demoralisation was completed by Britain's submission to the dictates of the International Monetary Fund in order to avoid economic collapse in 1976. In 1987 the historian Alan Sked wrote: 'Since 1967 the British seem to have lived in an era of perpetual economic crisis, fearing that growth will never permanently return and that absolute decline may be just around the corner. That period is still continuing.'[13]

Perception of economic and social decline is relative: living standards have continued to rise, but that perception is important. Since 1960, when the United Kingdom was still the most prosperous country in Europe, our relative position has steadily fallen. In terms of *per capita* income, by 1970 we were the tenth richest nation in the Organisation of Economic Co-Operation and Development; by 1983 we were the thirteenth, above only Italy, Ireland, Greece and Portugal. The price of ending the profoundly unsettling rise in inflation, which in 1975 reached twenty-four per cent has been recession and unemployment. In mid 1987 unemployment was officially three million, but effectively nearer four. Instead of modernisation, the country has undergone rationalisation, redundancies, and de-industrialisation.

Recession has encouraged the feeling that not only has the post-war period been one of decline, but that even its innovations have been a failure. There is a belief that the Welfare State has failed in education, health and the elimination of poverty. Some ten per cent of the population lives below the poverty line, a number being steadily added to by the long-term unemployed. The decline of industry has meant that dereliction has worsened. A 1986 study for the Department of the Environment warned 'the vast legacy of waste land in Britain is increasing, despite greater efforts of restoration', and there is nothing to suggest that urban wasteland will not continue to increase.[14] Recession has meant that the rate of loss of agricultural land to urban use has fallen, but it continues at about 45,000 acres a year.

The failure in housing has been symbolised by the demolition of tower blocks built only twenty years ago. The estimated cost of repairing the five million local authority houses in England and Wales (out of some twenty two million houses in the United Kingdom) is £20 billion. A million privately owned houses lack one or more basic amenity or are in need of repair. A million more are unfit for habitation. Examples of 'the boarded, tenantless flats, the fouled stairwells, the vandalised lifts, the endless graffiti' of Liverpool's 'putrescent housing', so graphically described by the former Secretary of State for the Environment, Michael Heseltine, can be found throughout Britain's major cities.[15]

The many failures of public housing and town planning have produced a crisis of confidence within the architectural profession, expressed in the bitterly contested election for the presidency of the Royal Institute of British Architects in 1986. The RIBA's 150th anniversary celebrations in 1984 were marred when, during a banquet at Hampton Court, the Prince of Wales attacked the plans for a proposed extension to the National Gallery as a 'monstrous carbuncle'. As a result the radically modernist design has been dropped in favour of sympathetic pastiche. Having delivered a serious blow to the reputation of modern architecture, the Prince has since moved on to criticise Britain's most advanced microchip factory as a 'high-tech version of a Victorian prison'.[16]

Decline has been most bitterly experienced in the inner cities where much of the black population is clustered. Immigration, at its peak in the early 1960s, has resulted in a black and Asian population of some two and a half million, a development that has altered the texture of urban life. Racial issues, such as an unemployment rate for blacks twice as high as for whites, have added to the social conflicts of the inner cities. The existence of an undeclared state of civil war in Northern Ireland has further damaged the United Kingdom's most depressed province, while bombing campaigns and consequently tighter security measures throughout Britain have added to the tension. Violent crime and theft are estimated to have quadrupled since the 1960s, and the police report steadily rising figures for all kinds of crime. Since the riots in Bristol in 1980 the crisis of social control has periodically led to pitched battles with the police, with race as a catalytic factor. The authorities have increased their powers of surveillance, the police are more frequently armed, and the underlying menace of violence is ritually reinforced by outbreaks of football hooliganism. Throughout 1984 the miners' strike dramatised the extent of social and economic conflict.

In the face of apparent decline and disintegration, it is not surprising that the past seems a better place. Yet it is irrecoverable, for we are condemned to live perpetually in the present. What matters is not the past, but our relationship with it. As individuals, our security and identity depend largely upon the knowledge we have of our personal and family history; the language and customs which govern our social lives rely for their meaning on a continuity between past and present.

Yet at times the pace of change, and its consequences, are so radical that not only is change perceived as decline, but there is the threat of total rupture with our past lives. 'We are saddened by the sight of an individual suffering amnesia,' write Tamara Hareven and Randolph Langenbach in *Our Past Before Us:*

> But we are often less concerned or aware when an entire community is subjected to what amounts to social amnesia as a result of massive clearance or alteration of the physical setting. The demolition of dwellings and factory buildings wipes out a significant chapter of the history of the place. Even if it does not erase them from local memory it tends to reduce or eliminate the recall of that memory, rendering less meaningful the communication of that heritage to a new generation. Such destruction deprives people of tangible manifestations of their identity.[17]

While a hold on the past is weakened, confidence in the value of the social identity that comes from a secure past is also undermined: 'the condemnation and clearance of physical structures can be read as a condemnation of the way of life which had been lived there.'[18]

The effect of such clearances has been vividly described by Elspeth King, curator of the People's Palace Museum in Glasgow: 'We've had the biggest area of comprehensive redevelopment in Europe, and it was like taking a rubber to the map and just rubbing places out and rebuilding them. People socially and indeed politically were very upset, and are trying to hang on to a bit of their past, and rediscover and explore their past.'[19]

Even without the sort of environmental changes that have taken place since 1945 it would have been necessary to adapt to the process of social change. A secure sense of identity depends not only on a confident location in time and place, but also on an ability to cope with the inevitable alterations that time brings about. The sense of time passing often evokes feelings of nostalgia but, it appears, nostalgia is one of the means we use to adjust to change.

In *Yearning for Yesterday: A Sociology of Nostalgia*, Fred Davis points out that nostalgia (literally, homesickness, a seventeenth-century medical term coined to describe the melancholia of Swiss mercenaries fighting abroad) is not simply a longing for the past, but a response to conditions in the present. Nostalgia is felt most strongly at a time of discontent, anxiety or disappointment, yet the times for which we feel nostalgia most keenly were often themselves periods of disturbance. Individually, it is common to experience a nostalgia for the pain and longing of late adolescence; collectively the Second

World War, and most particularly the Blitz, exercises a powerful hold on the British imagination, even for people who were not yet born in 1940. A cataclysmic event, such as the assassination of President Kennedy in 1963 serves as a focus of memory, and its recollection can trigger the release of waves of nostalgia which have little relation to the impact of the event itself.

Nostalgic memory should not be confused with true recall. For the individual, nostalgia filters out unpleasant aspects of the past, and of our former selves, creating a self-esteem that helps us to rise above the anxieties of the present. Collectively, nostalgia supplies the deep links that identify a particular generation; nationally it is the source of binding social myths. It secures, and it compensates, serving, according to Davis, 'as a kind of safety valve for disappointment and frustration suffered over the loss of prized values'.[20]

As the very act of publishing a sociology of nostalgia in 1979 implies, the nostalgic impulse has become significantly stronger in recent years. For Davis, 'the nostalgia wave of the Seventies is intimately related – indeed, the other side of the psychological coin, so to speak – to the massive identity dislocations of the Sixties.'[21] Writing in 1974 Michael Wood noted that 'the disease, if it is a disease, has suddenly become universal.' He stressed the contemporary longing for the past. 'What nostalgia mainly suggests about the present is not that it is catastrophic or frightening, but that it is undistinguished, unexciting, blank. There is no life in it, no hope, no future (the important thing about the present is what sort of a future it has). It is a time going nowhere, a time that leaves nothing for our imaginations to do except plunge into the past.'[22] Nostalgia can be a denial of the future.

Yet it is also a means of coping with change, with loss, with *anomie*, and with perceived social threat. It is around these unpleasant aspects of the present that our ideas of the past begin to coalesce. In 1978 Sir Roy Strong wrote:

> It is in times of danger, either from without or from within, that we become deeply conscious of our heritage. . . . within this word there mingle varied and passionate streams of ancient pride and patriotism, of a heroism in times past, of a nostalgia too for what we think of as a happier world which we have lost. In the 1940s we felt all this deeply because of the danger from without. In the 1970s we sense it because of the dangers from within. We are all aware of problems and troubles, of changes within the structure of society, of the dissolution of old values and standards. For the lucky few this may be exhilarating, even exciting, but for the majority it is confusing, threatening and dispiriting. The heritage represents some form of security, a point of reference, a

refuge perhaps, something visible and tangible which, within a topsy and turvy world, seems stable and unchanged. Our environmental heritage . . . is therefore a deeply stabilising and unifying element within our society.[23]

As this passage unconsciously reveals, nostalgia is profoundly conservative. Conservatism, with its emphasis on order and tradition, relies heavily on appeals to the authority of the past – typically in Mrs Thatcher's reference shortly before the 1983 general election to the recovery of 'Victorian values'. During the miners' strike she made much blunter political use of 'the enemy within'.

But nostalgia is a vital element in the myths of the Left as well as of the Right. There is a powerful myth of prelapsarian agricultural simplicity that has survived, even been encouraged by, three hundred years of industrialisation; the emergence of an urban proletariat has led to memories of community and class solidarity which are summoned up to confront contemporary conflicts and defeat. At times the myths of the past have become more powerful than mere party politics: the Royal Jubilee in 1976 and the Royal Wedding in 1981, albeit discreetly stage-managed as a ritual enactment of tribal loyalty, tapped the most atavistic roots. The Falklands War released profound emotions derived from folk memory – the uses to which the apparent rediscovery of a national identity were put is another matter.

The impulse to preserve the past is part of the impulse to preserve the self. Without knowing where we have been, it is difficult to know where we are going. The past is the foundation of individual and collective identity, objects from the past are the source of significance as cultural symbols. Continuity between past and present creates a sense of sequence out of aleatory chaos and, since change is inevitable, a stable system of ordered meanings enables us to cope with both innovation and decay. The nostalgic impulse is an important agency in adjustment to crisis, it is a social emollient and reinforces national identity when confidence is weakened or threatened.

The paradox, however, is that one of our defences against change is change itself: through the filter of nostalgia we change the past, and through the conservative impulse we seek to change the present. The question then is not whether or not we should preserve the past, but what kind of past we have chosen to preserve, and what that has done to our present.

BRIDESHEAD RE-REVISITED

In 1976 the mournful notes of a plangent, romantic theme tune introduced television audiences to the whispered messages of national loss and decay that echo through Evelyn Waugh's threnody on the decline and fall of the great house of Brideshead. This story of nostalgic sensuality, frustrated desires, corrupted principles and lost prospects was presented with all the splendour that costume drama can provide. The fictional places and identities of the novel took on material form: the magnificent palace of Castle Howard stood in for Brideshead, Lord Marchmain became Lord Olivier.

Actual locations took on a hyper-reality: Oxford University became a Gothic jewel in a Renaissance setting, its honey-coloured stones (refaced in the 1960s) glowing in the warm sunshine of late adolescent memory. Venice rose out of the mists of soft-focus in a sparkle of tiny waves, or a flash of fireworks over the Salute. The mere things of the Twenties and Thirties – motor cars, charabancs, steam trains – gleamed with brass and deep varnished paint. Dark polished wood, bright silver and the dense textures of tweed, linen and flannel evoked a rich material past made all the more desirable by the knowledge that, except in memory, all this was lost.

It was not entirely accidental that *Brideshead Revisited* should be adopted for television in the mid-Seventies, or that its episodes should be in production in 1974 and 1975. The Bridesheads of England were again under threat, just as they had been in 1944 when Evelyn Waugh completed the novel. The menace of 1944 was not foreign invasion and violent destruction, for there was no longer any danger that the war would be lost, but, after 'a bleak period of present privation and threatening disaster', there loomed what Waugh called 'the age of Hooper', a bleak featureless future governed by, and in the interests of, the all too common man.[1] Waugh looked gloomily towards a postwar world of mediocrity under a socialist government, whose policies meant that country houses and the values they represented would be swept away. But the country house has proved a more resilient element in British life than was feared in 1944 – and 1974.

Evelyn Waugh's novel demonstrates the peculiarly strong hold such places have on the British – though for once it seems more appropriate to say English – imagination. Because there has been no foreign invasion, civil war or revolution since the seventeenth century these houses both great and small represent a physical continuity which embodies the same adaptability to change within a respect for precedent and tradition that has shaped the common law. With a garden, a park and a greater or lesser estate, they enshrine the rural values that persist in a population that has been predominantly urban for more than a century. Some are works of art in themselves, but continuity, accumulation, even occasional periods of neglect, have meant that the furnishings and pictures of even minor houses have considerable historic and market value. As the great celebration of the country house at the National Gallery of Art in Washington in 1985–86 sought to demonstrate, 'they have become, as it were, vessels of civilization.'[2]

It seems only right that the catalogue of *The Treasure Houses of Britain* should open with a telescoped shot of Castle Howard that distorts the perspective and flattens the image as though it were on a television screen. An introductory evocation by the American director of the National Gallery in Washington, J. Carter-Brown luxuriates in the emotive chords such places strike:

> The mellow red brick of a Tudor manor house reflected in its moat; the domes and statues, cupolas and turrets, of one of Sir John Vanburgh's baroque palaces rising out of the mist; or the portico of a Palladian mansion seen across a lake at sunset, deer grazing by the water's edge. A deeply romantic picture this may be, painted in the golden light of Constable and Turner, but it shows what a central place the country house still holds in the British national consciousness, and what dreams of Elysium it continues to offer in an egalitarian twentieth century.[3]

Promoted by the British Council and sponsored by the Ford Motor Company, with the National Trust the largest single lender, *The Treasure Houses of Britain* displayed paintings, furniture, tapestries, silver and china from 200 houses in a series of rooms specially constructed to reflect the change – and continuity – of country house life. Opened by the Prince and Princess of Wales, it was, in the words of the *Economist*, 'a shameless sales pitch for the British heritage'. It was also, the article quoted one of the exhibition's backers as saying, no bad thing for NATO 'to be reminded occasionally of the civilization more directly at risk to Russia's SS–20s.'[4] The object of the sales pitch was to persuade American tourists to spend more of their £1 billion a year in Britain in country houses.

The country house is the most familiar symbol of our national heritage, a symbol which, for the most part has remained in private hands. That it has done so is a remarkable achievement in the face of the egalitarian twentieth century. It may well be that the century is less egalitarian than it might have been, not because the buildings and their contents have survived, but because of the values they enshrine. They are not museums – that is the whole basis on which they are promoted – but living organisms. As such they do not merely preserve certain values of the past: hierarchy, a sturdy individualism on the part of their owners, privilege tempered by social duty, a deference and respect for social order on the part of those who service and support them. They reinforce these values in the present. It is true that in some of the grander buildings adjustments to the twentieth century have had to be made, but the middle-scale houses continue much as before. The *National Trust Book of the English House* stresses: 'Unlike the great houses they still serve the needs of modern life as well as they served the needs of their builders. Their appeal is that they can be lived in; they remain essentially private even when they are open to visitors.'[5]

Sir Roy Strong has captured the sense of privacy of these national institutions exactly:

> We glimpse the park gates as we hurtle down a road, or we
> sense, behind some grey, mouldering stone wall, the magic of
> a landscape planting. Majestic trees pierce the skyline and a
> profusion of shrubs leads the eye through the artificial
> landscape in successive tantalising vistas. Alerted, we strain
> our eyes for a brief, fleeting glimpse of some noble pile
> floating in the distance, either embraced within some hollow
> or standing proud on a prominence.

Yet in spite of this charged description of the scenic voyeur, Strong continues: 'The ravished eyes stir the heart to emotion, for in a sense the historic houses of this country belong to everybody, or at least everybody who cares about this country and its traditions.'[6]

Such is the power of the cult of the country house. A building that can only be glimpsed becomes the erotic object of desire of a lover locked out. Yet he seems unaware of his exclusion. By a mystical process of identification the country house becomes the nation, and love of one's country makes obligatory a love of the country house. We have been re-admitted to paradise lost.

★ ★ ★

Re-admitted, that is, on visiting day. The country house is as much emblem as bricks and mortar, it has no formal architectural definition; consequently it is not possible to say how many country houses there are. The ideal house retains its contents, its parkland, at least the home estate – and its owners. The Historic Houses Association calculates that there are approximately 3,500 that retain their contents and supporting land, of which approximately 2,000 are in private hands and sustain a long-term family connection.

The uncertainty about the precise number of country houses reflects their privacy, and the fact that such houses, like their families, have come and gone ever since the Saxon settlements. If it is true that the country house is in decline, then it has been in decline for almost a century. It is certain that at least 1,116 country houses were demolished between 1875 and 1975 – though the disappearance of such places as Nonsuch Palace and Oatlands Park is a reminder that demolitions are nothing new. 1875 saw the beginnings of a long agricultural depression that lasted almost till the end of the century, and reduced the value of the great houses' supporting estates. In 1894 death duties were introduced, and although these were, to begin with, relatively light, the deaths of many heirs to estates as young officers in the First World War led to sometimes double and treble death duties being paid.

Between 1918 and 1945, 485 houses were demolished. The Thirties were years of economic depression, and with urbanisation the sources of agricultural and domestic labour began to dry up. On the outbreak of war in 1939 the government requisitioned virtually every country house for official purposes: for the storage of art works, as secret training establishments, laboratories, hospitals, or simply barracks. The Brideshead that Waugh's narrator revisits at the beginning of the novel, its park a shanty town of Nissen huts, the great fountain empty save for cigarette butts and barbed wire, the furniture in store and the rooms boarded up, faced a future that looked bleak indeed.

That the country house *has* survived is largely due to a private body, the National Trust. It is a private charity, governed by an executive committee appointed by a fifty-person council, of whom half are nominees from other amenity bodies. The Trust depends on donations, admission charges and the subscriptions of its members, and income from its farms and investments. Following a recruitment drive in recent years the membership stands at 1,400,000. In return for a basic subscription of £14.40 they gain free admission to National Trust properties, and have the right to vote for those Council members who are not appointed by related organisations, though most members are content to use their membership simply to visit Trust properties.

The National Trust is the largest private landowner in the United Kingdom, with (in December 1986) 540,000 acres, 470 miles of coastline, and 292 properties open to the public, 87 of them large houses. It owns 1,181 farms and some 15,000 agricultural buildings. The National Trust for Scotland owns 100,000 acres with 111 properties open to the public, including 19 castles and historic houses.

In spite of its status as a voluntary organisation, however, the Trust has long enjoyed a 'national' position, confirmed by a succession of National Trust Acts. This private body has a highly public function. While not directly funded by the government it has a special relationship with the Treasury, both as a repository for properties and objects that are given 'to the nation' in lieu of tax, and because it provides a form of tax haven for private estates which avoid tax by passing to the Trust. It is run by public figures, including members of Parliament and of the House of Lords, and has access to the government through that complex network of interlocking relationships and connections that make up the self-selected aristocracy of the Great and the Good. The formal links through its constitution with other amenity bodies are doubled by personal cross-memberships and common backgrounds in the field of public service. The Trust's present chairman, for instance, Dame Jennifer Jenkins, is married to the politician Roy Jenkins, and is the former chairman of the Consumers' Association, and of the Historic Buildings Council for England; she has also served on the Design Council, the management committee of the Courtauld Institute and the Ancient Monuments Board. A former secretary of the Ancient Monuments Society, she became its president in 1985. The Trust's director-general, Angus Stirling, is a former deputy secretary-general of the Arts Council and assistant director of the Paul Mellon Foundation for British Art. He is a director of the Royal Opera House and chairman of the Friends of Covent Garden. He has also served on the management committee of the Courtauld, sits on the Crafts Council and the executive committee of the London Symphony Orchestra and is a trustee of the Theatres Trust.

The National Trust has been described by one of its former chairmen, Lord Antrim, as 'a self-perpetuating oligarchy'[7]; in spite of its large membership it has long been the fiefdom of 'the amenity earls', or those who would like to live like them. In his contribution to *The Treasure Houses of Britain* Mark Girouard has described the attitude of generations of country house owners: 'An independent, property-owning landed class was seen as the right and natural ruling class, but their power and privileges were recognised as bringing corresponding duties.'[8] Such is the attitude inherited by the governors

55

of the National Trust. The Trust has the special status afforded to organisations that have been established for a long time. Yet it is not generally realised, that as it approaches its centenary, the National Trust is a quite different organisation to that which its founders intended.

The National Trust has its origins in the Commons, Open Spaces and Footpaths Preservation Society, founded in 1865, and its primary purpose was not the protection of buildings or private property, but public access to the countryside. As is now recognised, landowners regard their property as an asset to be exploited to the owner's best advantage; with rare exceptions, any sense of a responsibility to the general community who enjoy the landscape as a source of aesthetic refreshment is secondary. The conflict is clear in the battles to preserve access to common land against enclosures for farming which the Commons Preservation Society was formed to fight. Two of the Trust's founders, Octavia Hill and Canon Hardwicke Rawnsley had close connections with John Ruskin, whose writings, deeply conservative in origin, celebrated the beauties of the natural world and raged against the pillage and pollution of nineteenth-century capitalism. Canon Rawnsley led the Lake District Defence Society's resistance to the projection of railways through the Lakes with Ruskin's support, and Ruskin introduced Rawnsley to Octavia Hill, a prominent member of the Commons Preservation Society, whom he had helped with her schemes to improve working-class housing. In 1885 Rawnsley, Hill and the solicitor of the Commons Preservation Society Robert Hunter joined forces to protect the right of public access to the Lake District.

To the founders of the Trust, the landscape, especially that which expressed the spiritually regenerative forces of nature, rather than the civilising activities of man, was the primary value in danger. But memory, too, had a capacity for moral change, by acting as a reminder of former greatness, and the landscape could not be seen without its human associations. Accordingly, when the Trust was formally registered with the Board of Trade in January 1895 as a body intending to hold land in perpetuity, it was as 'The National Trust for Places of Historic Interest or Natural Beauty'.

The Trust's first acquisition was a stretch of headland above the resort of Barmouth in Wales, the small seed from which the Trust's continuing campaign to preserve the coastline through Enterprise Neptune has grown. It acquired its first house in 1896, the Clergy House at Alfriston, but this late fourteenth-century structure of timber, plaster and thatch exactly expresses the medievalising tastes of the first members. The purchase price was ten pounds. Other small buildings followed. The only acquisition that would qualify as a country house was the early sixteenth-century Barrington Court in 1907. In that year the Trust's inevitable responsibility for buildings as well as land was officially recognised, if only in parenthesis, by the first National Trust Act, which empowered it to promote 'the permanent preservation for the benefit of the nations lands and tenements (including buildings) of beauty or historic interest'. The Act introduced the concept that the Trust's property was 'inalienable', that is to say it could never be disposed of or taken away from the Trust, even by compulsory purchase, except by express will of Parliament. Many of the early properties acquired were small, but there were important protective acquisitions in the Lake District, and by 1914 the Trust controlled 5,500 acres.

While the early members of the National Trust, 725 in 1914, cannot be said to have been promoters of the cult of the country house, they were sympathetic to the cult of the countryside which expressed itself in the Arts and Crafts movement, and the idealisation of rural values felt by an increasingly urbanised population. This vicarious enjoyment of the countryside was cunningly exploited by the magazine publisher Edward Hudson, who bought a not very successful paper, *Racing Illustrated*, and relaunched it in 1897 as *Country Life*. The magazine was a skilful mixture of traditional aristocratic values with the open air principles of the reformed public schools. It combined farming, field sports and golf with articles on society figures, fashion and interior decoration. Alongside articles on the new recreation of motoring came discussions of dying rural crafts.

Since the country house is central to this gentry's eye view of rural existence, *Country Life* naturally featured country houses in its pages, and the magazine became the obvious place for estate agents to advertise such properties, which were coming more frequently onto the market as a result of the agricultural depression and the effect of death duties. *Country Life* made Hudson rich, and although he himself was never particularly comfortable as a countryman, Hudson commissioned work on no less than three important houses: Deanery Garden, Plumpton Place and the restored Lindisfarne Castle. They were all the work of Edwin Lutyens, whose romantic use of brick, tile and wood set a style which, infinitely debased, is the source of the rural echoes in the lead panes of stockbroker Tudor and the false timbering of subtopian pre-war estates. Naturally, Lutyens was regularly featured in the pages of *Country Life*.

The magazine continues to play a central role in the promotion and protection of the country house. Its long series of scholarly articles on individual houses, begun by its architectural editor Christopher Hussey, who worked for the magazine from 1920 until his death in 1970, are an important source of knowledge. Under Hussey, *Country Life* began a seven-volume history of the country house, and Hussey's successors as architectural editor – Mark Girouard, John Cornforth, Marcus Binney and Clive Aslet – form an influential group of architectural writers. Marcus Binney, editor of *Country Life* from 1984 to 1986, was the founder of SAVE Britain's Heritage, and is now its president. The present architectural editor, Clive Aslet, is secretary of the Thirties Society.

In the 1920s, as the original founders of the National Trust began to die off, the focus of policy started to shift. Short of funds, it was no longer eager to accept any parcel of land however small, while the impact of death duties on the great estates became a cause of alarm. In 1923 the Trust formally begged the Chancellor of the Exchequer to grant tax concessions to owners of important country houses to help them keep their properties in good repair – the first of a succession of pleas which continues to the present day – though without success. In 1931, however, the Treasury conceded an important change in the tax laws as an incentive to landowners to give property to the Trust. The 1931 Finance Act allowed land or buildings given to the Trust to escape death duties; owners or their heirs could reduce their tax liabilities by judicious gifts to the Trust, and thus keep the rest of the estate intact, while the Trust stood to gain considerable land and buildings. In 1937 the exemption was extended to cases where the donor retained a life interest in the property.

The National Trust began to adapt to the new circumstances. In 1932 it acquired a new chairman, the Marquess of Zetland, a former governor of Bengal, who had had no previous experience of the Trust, but who had the aristocratic connections that would give the Trust access to the owners of great estates who might see the advantages of passing land to the Trust. The emphasis was still on land, but at the Trust's annual general meeting in 1934 the Marquess of Lothian proposed that the Trust should adopt a positive policy for the acquisition of country houses, and press for the creation of a fiscal scheme that would ensure their survival. In 1936 a Country House Committee was established, with the architectural writer James Lees-Milne as secretary. The Trust again failed to secure the tax advantages it would have liked country house owners to have had, but in 1937 a fresh National Trust Act confirmed the Trust's new role as the protector of the country house.

The terms under which the 1907 Act had permitted the holding of buildings 'of beauty or historic interest' were altered to 'national interest or architectural, historic or artistic interest', and for the first time the Trust's responsibilities were extended to furniture and pictures. The Trust was empowered to hold land and investments purely in order to generate an income that would enable it to preserve and maintain properties. Local authorities were empowered to give land or buildings to the Trust, or to contribute to the acquisition and maintenance of Trust buildings. Finally, the Act permitted the Trust to protect land or buildings it did not own by making covenants with the owners, by which the owner agreed not to fell timber or alter his buildings without the agreement of the Trust. The land did not change hands, and there was no condition giving public right of access, but the existence of the covenant did reduce the owner's liability to death duties. As a result of the 1937 Act the Trust was able formally to launch its Country House Scheme.

The essence of the scheme was that wherever possible the Trust arranged for the owners to continue living in the house, either as tenants on a long lease, or under the terms of what is known as a 'memorandum of wishes', which is not legally enforceable, but gives the owner long-term security for himself and his heirs. Thus, in exchange for often quite limited rights of access to the public, the owner was able to continue his life very much as before, without the financial burden of maintaining the house in which he lived.

This extension of the power and influence of the National Trust coincided with a shift in the tastes of those influential within it. Before the early Thirties most of the buildings it had shown interest in were medieval or Tudor and Jacobean. The only country house it acquired in the 1930s, Montacute in Somerset in 1931, dates from the late sixteenth century. But, partially because of the threat to later country houses resulting from the depression, and redevelopment in London, such as the demolition of Robert Adam's Adelphi Terrace in 1937, the architecture of the eighteenth century began to acquire a new value in the experts' eyes. The Society for the Protection of Ancient Buildings could hold no brief for neo-classical architecture: accordingly, the Georgian Group came into being in 1937.

Its first chairman was Lord Derwent, a member of the National Trust, and its membership included James Lees-Milne, secretary of the Trust's new Country House Scheme, Christopher Hussey from *Country Life*, the furniture expert Lord Gerald Wellesley (later, the seventh Duke of Wellington), and the architects Claud Phillimore and Albert Richardson, both of whom continued to build in Georgian style. Richardson's devotion to the eighteenth century was such that he claimed to read only eighteenth-century newspapers. The Georgian Group was the focus of a revival of interest in the architecture of 1714–1830 which continues to this day; the Group sits with the Trust on the Joint Committee of National Amenity Societies, and administers the Cleary Fund for the maintenance and preservation of Georgian Buildings.

By 1939 the Trust's holdings had increased to 410 properties and 58,900 acres. In 1940, on the death of Lord Lothian, the original proponent of the scheme, the Trust acquired Blickling in Norfolk, its first property under the Country House Scheme. The need to preserve and record what was now perceived as an expression of the civilised values for which the country was fighting had become urgent.

Throughout the war the National Trust steadily acquired important properties. Invalided out of the army in 1941, the scheme's secretary, James Lees-Milne toured the country, inspecting potential properties and talking to their owners. He kept a private diary, subsequently published, which is remarkably frank about the camp and snobbish values he brought to his work, and which he clearly shared with other members of the Trust. He records the comment of a colleague during the arrangements for the furnishing of Montacute House in 1946, who 'remarked that the public could not of course be admitted to the house because they smelt.'[9]

For the most part, James Lees-Milne's diaries are a melancholy account of decay, of elderly owners stranded in the hulks of their houses after the tide of social change had swept them aside and beached them, without the staff to run them or the funds to keep them afloat. The damage done by enemy action that he records is more than equalled by the wanton destruction of official and unofficial vandals. There were many Bridesheads in 1944. By the end of the war the Trust had acquired Wallington, Cliveden, Great Chatfield, Polesden Lacy, Speke Hall, West Wycombe and Lacock Abbey among other properties, so that in 1945 it controlled 112,000 acres and was responsible for nearly a hundred historic buildings.

★ ★ ★

As the age of Hooper dawned in 1945, Britain seemed on the verge of a social revolution. The new Labour government was busy nationalising the mines and the railways, increasing taxes, rationing luxuries and substituting a bureaucratic order and equality for the old system of social privilege and respect. Country house owners and their allies viewed this new world with suspicion, none more so than James Lees-Milne, as he surveyed the contents of Brockhampton House, which had passed to the Trust on the death of its last owner in 1946:

> This evening the whole tragedy of England impressed itself upon me. This small, not very important seat in the heart of our secluded country, is now deprived of its last squire. A whole social system has broken down. What will replace it beyond government by the masses, uncultivated, rancorous, savage, philistine, the enemies of all things beautiful? How I detest democracy. More and more I believe in benevolent autocracy.[10]

The new régime however did not prove to be entirely philistine. The 1947 Town and Country Planning Act, for all its faults (which favoured landowners), remains the foundation for our present system of land use. It introduced the concept of green belts, and sought to improve on the principle, first introduced in the Town and Country Planning Act of 1944, that specific buildings, graded according to architectural merit, should be listed, and therefore protected from demolition or alteration without local authority – or, on appeal, government – consent. Local authorities were empowered to issue building preservation orders for the first time.

The Labour government was also sympathetic to the plight of the country house: in 1946 the Chancellor of the Exchequer, Hugh Dalton, decided to use powers that had lain virtually dormant since they were first created in 1910, to accept property in lieu of tax in such a way as to be able to hand the houses or land on to the National Trust or other suitable bodies. Since such exchanges in kind meant a loss of cash tax revenue, he established the National Land Fund with £50 million raised from the sale of war surplus, from which it would be possible to compensate the government for the loss of cash. The Fund was intended as a memorial to all those who had lost their lives in the war; the money was invested in government stock to provide the Fund with a recurrent income, but its administration was left to the Treasury, rather than independent trustees, and although, in the next twenty years, the National Trust acquired twenty-six properties through the fund, it was not used to the extent that Dalton intended.

While ready to accept houses from the Fund, the National Trust was anxious that its independence would not be compromised by too close cooperation with the government. Part of the difficulty was that if the government accepted a house in lieu of tax, and then passed it on to the Trust, the owners were in a less favourable position to negotiate the terms on which they could continue to live in the property. Further, while the National Land Fund could pass houses on to the National Trust, it was not allowed to endow them with the income that such buildings required for their proper maintenance. The rapid expansion of the Trust's holdings during and immediately after the war presented the Trust with a severe problem: it held a rich store of land and buildings, but it was short of the revenue to restore or maintain them. During the 1930s its lands had enjoyed a benevolent neglect – thus creating an almost accidental group of nature reserves – but from 1945 there was an urgent need to generate income from its agricultural land and modernise the farms let to tenants. Only donations and special appeals kept the Trust ahead of a series of annual deficits.

At the best of times the Trust could only cope with a limited number of rescue operations, and it became increasingly wary of accepting houses without an endowment of land or investments that could ensure their upkeep. In the late 1940s, as demolitions continued, the country house seemed more endangered than ever. Many needed major repairs following their wartime occupation; owners who had moved out in 1939 had neither the means nor the inclination to move back in again; building licenses were at a premium. Country houses were being taken over by schools, nursing homes, and even prisons. The Labour government recognised that there was a growing problem, and in 1948 appointed a committee under Sir Ernest Gowers to investigate.

The Gowers Report on *Houses of Outstanding Historic or Architectural Interest* (1950) concluded that 'owing to the economic and social changes we are faced with a disaster comparable only to that which the country suffered by the Dissolution of the Monasteries in the sixteenth century.'[11] The report strongly favoured private ownership, and recommended a number of tax changes that would improve their chances of survival. In the event, only one of the Gowers recommendations passed into law, although it was to be of substantial benefit to the Trust. In 1953 the Historic Buildings and Monuments Act established quasi-independent Historic Buildings Councils for England, Scotland and Wales with government funds to assist in the repair of historic buildings. Private owners qualified if they could prove financial need, and they were expected to reciprocate by granting a measure of public access to their properties. The National

Trust quickly became a major recipient of Historic Buildings Council funds.

Although the failure to implement all the recommendations of the Gowers report was a disappointment, the position of the country house began to improve. Demolitions reached their peak in 1955, when seventy-six were lost, but after that declined rapidly. The steady rise in the value of agricultural land and of investments in the stock market over the next decade meant that fewer owners felt their homes to be an insupportable burden. In 1955 the present Duke and Duchess of Devonshire decided that they would move back into the great house of Chatsworth.

Some owners enterprisingly recognised that it was possible to secure their future by satisfying the public's increasing curiosity about the great houses, and (continuing a tradition that goes back to the eighteenth century) open them to the public and charge admission. The pioneer was the Marquess of Bath, who opened Longleat in 1949, followed by Lord Montagu of Beaulieu in 1952 and the Duke of Bedford at Woburn Abbey in 1955. It was quickly recognised that it was not enough simply to open the doors: there had to be an attraction, so the lions were installed at Longleat, the motor cars at Beaulieu, and nudist camps and jazz festivals held at Woburn. The age of marketing the heritage had begun: the secret of such houses was that they were marketed as stately *homes*.

The country house was not only financially, but culturally more secure. During the period of post-war austerity the nostalgic note struck by *Brideshead Revisited* in 1945 had become a popular refrain. Plays and novels set in country houses were a stable source of entertainment, and with the increase in car ownership, visiting National Trust and other properties became a popular recreation. The novelist Nigel Dennis satirised the British obsession with the pre-war world of the country house in *Cards of Identity* (1955): 'This sort of house was once a heart and centre of the national identity. A whole world lived in relation to it. Millions knew who they were by reference to it. Hundreds of thousands look back at it, and not only grieve for its passing but still depend on it, non-existent though it is, to tell them who they are. Thousands who never knew it are taught every day to cherish its memory and to believe that without it no man will be able to tell his whereabouts again.'[12]

The truth was, however, that society had re-oriented itself in relation to the values that the country house represented: nostalgia for the past ensured the continuation of the country house into the present. The National Trust played an important role, not only in taking a significant number of houses into its care, but by changing the perception of country house ownership from one of privileged

63

possession (though that of course had its own snobbish appeal) to one of responsible guardianship. The social historian Noel Annan had the National Trust, as well as the British Council, the Arts Council and the BBC in mind when he discussed the influence of 'The Intellectual Aristocracy' in an essay of that title in 1955. 'The pro-consular tradition and the English habit of working through established institutions and modifying them to meet social needs only when such needs are proven are traits strongly exhibited by the intelligentsia of this country. Here is an aristocracy, secure, established and, like the rest of English society, accustomed to responsible and judicious utterance and sceptical of iconoclastic speculation.'[13]

The effect of the judicious modifications to the social and economic role of country house ownership, which the National Trust had helped to bring about, was acknowledged by Evelyn Waugh, when he issued a revised version of *Brideshead Revisited* in 1959:

> It was impossible to foresee, in the spring of 1944, the
> present cult of the English country house. It seemed then
> that the ancestral seats which were our chief national artistic
> achievement were doomed to decay and spoilation like the
> monasteries in the sixteenth century. So I piled it on rather,
> with passionate sincerity. Brideshead today would be open to
> trippers, its treasures rearranged by expert hands and the
> fabric better maintained than it was by Lord Marchmain.
> And the English aristocracy has maintained its identity to a
> degree that then seemed impossible.[14]

The rescue of so many Bridesheads placed a considerable strain on the finances of the Trust, and there were those who questioned not only the wisdom, but the morality of the Country House Scheme. Appropriately, the opposition in the 1960s was led by the son of one of the Trust's founders, a retired naval commander, Conrad Rawnsley. In response to criticisms that it was neglecting its original purposes, in 1963 the Trust decided to launch Enterprise Neptune, a special appeal to enable it to take into care as much of the unspoiled coastline as possible. Rawnsley was placed in charge of the appeal, but according to the Trust's official history he 'found it difficult to work in harmony with the Executive Committee or gain the confidence of his colleagues on the staff', and in 1966, following a series of internal rows, Rawnsley was sacked.[15]

Rawnsley however fought back through the constitution by calling a costly Extraordinary General Meeting and a poll of members. Constitutional wrangling is an expensive business, and although Rawnsley was defeated, the Trust commissioned a high powered accountant, Sir Henry (now Lord) Benson to head an enquiry into the Trust. When the Benson Report appeared in 1968 it confirmed the strain the most recent acquisitions had imposed – there was a backlog of four and three quarter million pounds' worth of repairs to be done on properties – and urged that future agreements with owners should allow greater public access. But the administrative changes he proposed were a victory for the amenity Earls. The function of the executive committee as an inner cabinet was confirmed, and the calling of polls and extraordinary meetings made more difficult for the ordinary member.

The Executive Committee can still be challenged by the Trust's members. In 1982 it faced another Extraordinary General Meeting as a result of its decision to lease twelve acres of land on the Bradenham Estate to the Ministry of Defence for the extension of an underground command centre. Although overwhelmingly defeated, the protestors were able to argue that the concept of inalienability of National Trust land did not seem to apply when it came to the Ministry of Defence.

The consequences of the Country House Scheme have now come into conflict with the more recent growth of an environmental lobby, which argues that the financial needs of the Trust's houses have caused it to neglect its primary responsibility to the landscape. (At the 1986 AGM the Trust's properties in the Lake District were a particular focus of discontent.) As the largest private landowner in the country, the Trust generates an income of £7.7 million a year from 1,100 tenanted farms, and as we have seen, commercial farming methods have radically altered in the last twenty years. In 1985 the British Association of Nature Conservationists attemped an assessment of the Trust's performance.

The authors of the report acknowledged that some Trust properties do receive good nature conservation management, but other areas of conservation interest had 'while in the possesion of the National Trust, been destroyed or seriously degraded.' They challenge the National Trust's priorities:

> Although conservation is now accepted as desirable, the land
> is still seen primarily as a source of income. Wherever
> possible the estate makes money for the maintenance of the
> organisation and the built properties. Within the Trust there
> is an appreciation of fine houses and their content: there is
> even an acceptance of the need to conserve the urban
> commonplace. In contrast, there is no apparent level of
> appreciation and zest for conservation in the rural estate.
> This attitude reflects the composition of the leadership of the
> Trust.

Their conclusion is that 'in many respects the Trust has failed in its function to resist the destruction of the rural beauties its founders were so passionately concerned about.'[16]

The chairman of the National Trust, Dame Jennifer Jenkins, has dismissed the conservationists' report as 'a wholly unacceptable and unproven attack on the Trust.'[17] The Trust continues to hold a secure position as the repository and expression of cultural values that are distinctly British: a respect for privacy and private ownership, and a disinclination to question the privileges of class. In the shadow of the Trust, private owners have been able to claim to be doing no more than carrying on the Trust's work at their own expense. The cult of the country house has ensured their survival – even when in 1974 the call to arms sounded again.

As is well known, the unsteady boom of the Sixties ground to a halt at the end of the decade and the stock market began to fall, while inflation drove wages and prices spiralling upwards. Country house owners were affected like everyone else, but from 1972 onwards alarming rumours began to circulate that the Labour Party – out of office since 1970 – intended to introduce a tax on capital and assets that would forcibly carry out the redistribution of wealth that, in spite of a top rate of income tax of ninety-eight per cent had failed to occur since 1945. In March 1974 Labour was returned to power, and in August published a green paper outlining proposals both for a wealth tax on current capital, and a capital transfer tax to replace death duty.

The wealth tax would be an annual tax on assets, including houses worth £100,000 or more, and would take in securities, life insurance, copyrights, patents and all but minor works of art. (House prices have risen so much since then that it is important to remember that the government originally calculated that the tax would be paid by only one per cent of the population.) The government was well aware that for those people whose wealth largely consisted of works of art, collections of books or other objects of cultural significance the only way to pay the tax would be by selling off part of the collection, and accordingly it was prepared to consider exemption in the same way that exemptions already existed from death duty. The green paper also acknowledged that historic houses faced a similar difficulty. 'The government recognise the danger that the wealth tax could lead to the dispersal of the national heritage: they intend to ensure that this does not happen and that instead our heritage becomes more readily available to the public generally.'[18]

66

This assurance was hardly sufficient for those who might have to pay such a tax. The threat to the heritage from a wealth tax was used to justify resistance to the tax altogether. Even before the green paper was published opposition to the idea had found a focus in the formation of a campaign committee, Heritage in Danger. The prime mover was the fine art dealer Hugh Leggatt, around whose 'ample luncheon table' the campaign against the wealth tax was co-ordinated. (The phrase comes from Patrick Cormack's *Heritage in Danger*. In the second edition the 'ample' has disappeared.)[19] Opposition to the tax proved almost universal, and a Parliamentary Select Committee appointed to consider the scheme heard a stream of witnesses including the Country Landowners Association, the Historic Houses Association, the British Tourist Authority, the National Art Collections Fund, the Standing Commission on Museums and Galleries, the Trustees of the National Gallery, Tate Gallery and the British Museum, and the Reviewing Committee on the Export of Works of Art all express alarm at the potential consequences. The National Trust spoke up for the private owner. It told the committee 'The National Trust's anxieties arise from the fear that private owners, in whose ownership the bulk of the national heritage at present lies, may be forced by the new taxes and inflation to dispose of their property and that as a result the national heritage will be greatly reduced or dispersed.'[20]

Shortly before the Select Committee reported in December 1975 a petition against the tax, bearing a million signatures gathered in at country houses during the summer, was presented to Parliament. The only voices in favour of the tax came from a small group of left-wing art critics, and the Labour government's Minister for the Arts, Hugh Jenkins.

It is impossible not to conclude that the campaign against the wealth tax was a powerful stimulus to the spread of the word 'heritage'. 1975 was indeed to be European Architectural Heritage Year, but Heritage in Danger proved a powerful rallying cry for the wealth tax lobby, and a number of projects associated with Architectural Heritage Year were recruited to the campaign.

One such was a report by the architectural writer John Cornforth commissioned in 1972 by the Historic Houses Committee of the British Tourist Authority, a committee of country house owners which became the foundation of the Historic Houses Association in 1973. When Cornforth's report was published with the help of *Country Life* in the Autumn of 1974 the wealth tax debate was at its height, and it was appropriately titled *Country Houses in Britain – Can They Survive?* Cornforth's answer was that they could, provided that they were allowed to live in a favourable tax climate.

Publication of Cornforth's report coincided with an exhibition at the Victoria and Albert Museum which his research had helped to inspire. Although the Minister for the Arts, Hugh Jenkins, was able to force Sir Roy Strong – technically a civil servant – to resign from Heritage in Danger, there was nothing he could do to stop the V&A's director from mounting an exhibition that spoke powerfully for the country house lobby. *The Destruction of the Country House: 1875–1975* gave the impression that the private country house was about to disappear altogether. The exhibition began with an evocative roll call of the one thousand and more that had gone in the past century, including 250 since the war, and Sir Roy Strong's catalogue essay painted a bitter picture of the rising costs of insurance, Value Added Tax, security and staffing. 'Country house owners are the hereditary custodians of what was one of the most vital forces of cultural creation in our history.' Throughout the catalogue the impression is given that while the National Trust had saved more than a hundred houses, it had not saved the life that went with it. 'In nearly every instance the family ultimately abandoned the house,' claimed Sir Roy, somewhat erroneously. 'Death duties, and capital gains tax, let alone the threatened forms of Wealth and Inheritance Taxes, spell the final ruin of these most precious works of art.' It was in this context that he wrote 'the historic houses of this country belong to everybody, or at least everybody who cares about this country and its traditions.'[21]

The same message was hammered home in Patrick Cormack's *Heritage in Danger*, first published in 1976, and reissued – with adjustments – in 1978, after it had formed the basis for a television series. 'It is a sobering thought that more houses are now under siege than at any time since the Civil War, though the weapons menacing them are fiscal rather than military, and those directing them are Government forces.'[22] The last clause was dropped in the later edition. Cormack was particularly anxious to deny the allegations of 'numerous agitatory articles' that a wealth tax would be welcome to those who speculated in art.[23] The reason that dealers objected to the wealth tax proposals was that a sudden rush of sales to meet the tax might swamp the market, and that London's role as the centre of the world's art market would be destroyed.

But by 1976 the wealth tax was a dead letter. Although it was never officially abandoned, when in December 1975 the Parliamentary Select Committee failed to agree, and produced no fewer than five rival draft reports, it was clear that the heritage campaign had succeeded. Hugh Jenkins lost his post as Minister for the Arts a few months later. If anything the position of country house owners was improved by the Capital Transfer Tax Act of 1975 which gave exemptions to houses where owners permitted them to open to the public for a minimum of sixty days, and exempted agricultural land which the owner farmed himself. It also permitted the setting up of private charitable trusts as a complete haven for houses and supporting land. The wealth tax drew its last gasp in the run up to the 1979 general election: Heritage in Danger warned that £200 million worth of art and books would go on the market if the tax were introduced. When the Chancellor Denis Healey replied that it was no longer considered practical to apply the tax to works of art, but that no decision had been taken on historic houses, the chairman of the Historic Houses Association, George Howard, owner of the television Brideshead, Castle Howard, warned that Labour's election manifesto meant that there would be no more privately owned historic houses. The wealth tax disappeared with the defeat of the Labour government.

Although Brideshead, once more at the centre of the national consciousness thanks to television, was safe from the menace of the wealth tax, nowhere in the United Kingdom was it possible to escape the effects of the economic crisis of the mid-Seventies. The Department of the Environment, which had first encouraged local authorities to participate in Architectural Heritage Year in 1975, found itself imposing cuts in a desperate attempt to save money. The following year a hard pressed government found itself with a heritage issue of embarrassing proportions.

Though a short-term defeat, the battle of Mentmore Towers led to a significant victory for the heritage lobby. In 1974 the Seventh Earl of Rosebery was faced with a considerable tax bill on the death of his father. In order to retain the family estate at Dalmeny intact he offered another property, Mentmore, built and furnished in high Victorian style by Baron Mayer de Rothschild, in lieu of death duties. The valuation first put on the house and its contents for tax purposes was two million pounds. Such a transaction was a prime candidate for Hugh Dalton's National Land Fund, but certain changes had taken place in the circumstances of the Fund since it had been established in 1946.

The Land Fund had never been fully put to the uses for which Dalton had intended it, to the extent that by 1954 it had spent only a little over £900,000, out of the income from £50 million. In 1957 the Treasury proposed that as so little of the income was being spent, most of the capital sum should be transferred to the general government balance. The case for this was presented by the Financial Secretary to the Treasury at the time, Mr Enoch Powell, a man who has since made a reputation as the defender of the purity of racial heritage. He argued, somewhat casuistically, that since the fund was controlled by the Treasury and invested in government stocks, the government had merely lent money to itself and the Land Fund 'until it comes to be used for any particular purpose, is non-existent; not merely inert, it is absolutely non-existent.'[24] In the face of Mr Powell's withering logic, the capital of the Fund was reduced to £10 million.

In spite of this reduction, the annual income of the Fund in 1974 was approaching two million pounds, but the Labour government, facing a public expenditure crisis of huge proportions, produced a new argument. Any expenditure by the Fund would constitue part of general government spending, and therefore would count against the public sector borrowing requirement. Accordingly, the government could only offer Lord Rosebery a million pounds. The haggling went on into 1976, by which time the tax bill had risen to three million. Finally Lord Rosebery lost patience, and in May 1977 Sothebys' held a sale at Mentmore. Before the sale the government agreed to accept four pieces of furniture in lieu of £1 million in tax, but the sale of the contents of Mentmore alone raised £6 million. The house itself changed hands for an undisclosed sum, and is now a centre for transcendental meditation. The National Gallery, which had urged the government to accept a portrait of Madame de Pompadour by Francois-Hubert Drouais as part of the tax settlement, had to find £385,000 out of an annual purchase grant of £990,000 in order to acquire the painting.

As a result of the Mentmore *débâcle* a Select Committee of the House of Commons was established to enquire into the whole functioning of the Land Fund. It reported in March 1978, recommending that the Fund be re-established – with its original capital – under independent trustees. Although the Treasury civil servants prevaricated, the government replied with a white paper accepting most of the committee's proposals in February 1979, but the general election in May meant that it was a Conservative government which finally introduced a National Heritage Bill in the Autumn. The full £50 million was not restored. The Fund was re-established as the National Heritage Memorial Fund with £12.4 million, to be topped up by annual grants from the Department of the Environment and the Office of Arts and Libraries, but it was handed over to the control of a chairman and ten independent trustees, described by the Arts Minister Norman St John Stevas as 'cultured generalists', who would be appointed by the Prime Minister.[25] The heritage had achieved a new legislative status, protected by a quango empowered to make grants or loans to preserve not just buildings, but any land or object which, in the opinion of the trustees, is of outstanding scenic, historic, aesthetic or scientific interest. The word Memorial, the source of

Hugh Dalton's inspiration, was only added after an amendment in the House of Lords.

In the 1980s country houses have become more than ever symbols of continuity and security, as *The National Trust Book of the English House* (1985) reminds us: 'They look back to periods of apparent stability and order that, to some people, seem preferable to the chaos of the present.'[26] The National Trust's role as the guardian of this order has been acknowledged by its present director-general, Angus Stirling, who wrote in his 1985 report 'The concept of benefit deriving from the Trust's care of much of the country's finest landscape and buildings has special significance at this time, when the nation is so troubled by the effect of unemployment, the deprivation of inner cities and the rapidity of change in society.'[27]

Although the Country Landowners' Association and the Historic Houses Association now also exist as lobbies for the protection of private ownership, the Trust still sees its function as protecting owners as well as houses, as Stirling's report makes clear: 'The Trust prefers to see historic houses remain in the ownership of the families who cared for them in the past, and therefore continues actively to support legislation designed to make that possible. The fiscal climate for the private owner is at present somewhat better than it was ten years ago and it is reasonable to hope that the number of houses being offered to the Trust may reduce.'[28]

Throughout the post-war period the country house has retained a central position as one of the definitive emblems of the British cultural tradition – principally through appeals to its 'national' significance in the face of economic threat. The National Trust's commitment to the continued occupation of houses for whom it accepts responsibility by the families that formerly owned them has preserved a set of social values as well as dining chairs and family portraits. Some sixty National Trust properties retain accommodation of some kind for the family of their original donors. That these houses are therefore not perceived as museums is presented as a great virtue. The Trust's policy is to show objects 'in their natural setting and in the ambience of the past.'[29] But the 'ambience of the past' raises questions of definition and interpretation: a museum has as its objective not just the preservation of evidences of the past but the interpretation of that evidence to the present, yet this is precisely what the National Trust approach refuses to do.

Even when the facts of history mean that a house cannot be lived in because the line has died out, it is still presented, in the view of the Trust's chief expert on interior decoration in the Fifties and Sixties, so that it 'should look like one where the family had just gone out for the afternoon.'[30] This suggests that history is treated, not as a process of development and change, but something achieved on arrival at the present day. However scholarly the presentation of each item, there is an implicit decision to present the house and its history in the best possible light. The director of the National Trust's Youth Theatre fell straight into this trap in 1986 when his troupe arrived at Hanbury Hall: 'The house has rather a tragic history of broken marriages and suicide; but we chose to jolly it up a bit and have Emma Vernon's coming-out party with her mum looking for a suitable suitor. So it was all about blokes (in a totally random selection of looney period costumes) vying for the pretty heiress with the cash – again a fairly universal theme.'[31]

It is the Trust's present policy to concentrate more on the acquisition of open countryside and coastline – Enterprise Neptune was relaunched in 1985 – and in the case of country houses act 'only as a safety net when other solutions have been explored.'[32] The focus is now on the smaller, vernacular buildings on its estates, but this has not meant that it has ceased to acquire major new responsibilities: Calke Abbey in 1984, Nostell Priory and Kedleston Hall in 1986. Now that the public's taste has shifted towards a nostalgia for the everyday, the Trust is opening the kitchens as well as the state rooms. Calke Abbey is a case in point. The house, acquired with the help of £5 million from the National Heritage Memorial Fund, is not architecturally especially distinguished, but it had not been touched for years, and its rooms were stuffed with the relics of pre-war life. Calke Abbey is to be treated 'as a document of social history, complete with its kitchens and laundries, stables and riding school, joiner's and blacksmith's shops, church and park – a quintessence of all that is magical about English country house life.'[33] A life not just preserved, but revived.

Part of the magic of the country house is that the privilege of private ownership has become a question of national prestige. Those who have held on to their houses, and the majority of all country houses remain in private hands, have had to concede a greater degree of public access in exchange for tax exemptions and repair grants, others have turned their historic houses into commercial enterprises, but the hierarchy of cultural values that created the country houses remains the same. Private ownership has been elided into a vague conception of public trusteeship. The Earl of March, prominent during the wealth tax campaign, has said of his successful enterprise at Good-wood House in Sussex: 'I never feel that I am the owner – only a steward for my lifetime, and not principally for the benefit of the family but for the whole community.'[34]

One of the best ways to stimulate public concern, as did *The Destruction of the Country House*, is to claim that the object of concern is about to disappear for ever. The campaign on behalf of the country house has been so successful that it is more flourishing now than at any time in the last century. The capital and incomes of private owners are in a much healthier tax position, as the National Trust confirms, and it turns out that, far from the country house disappearing, more than 200 new ones have been built since the war.

This information comes in a fascinating survey by the architectural historian John Martin Robinson, *The Latest Country Houses*. The book is, in a sense, a reply to Clive Aslet's earlier survey of the period up to 1939, *The Last Country Houses*.[35] Robinson writes: 'The subject could almost be subtitled "furtive house-building" as the owners have not been particularly keen to draw attention to their enterprise in this field.'[36] The book challenges claims of crisis and decay that have been made on behalf of the country house owner. 'The traditional land-owner has maintained a surprisingly active role in local life and fulfils a function not dissimilar from that of the constitutional monarch in national life, still acting as the focus of social, ceremonial and charitable activities in his area. Above all his estates have survived as viable economic and social units.'[37]

While country house life has continued independently of the Welfare State, and its scions continue to supply the media with its staple diet of fashion and scandal, the growth of tourism has created a fresh source of revenue, and the phenomenal rise in the price of works of art – so alarming to public institutions concerned for the heritage – has been a discreet source of funds. Robinson comments, 'At least three of the new country houses described in this book (the reader must guess which) were paid for largely out of the proceeds of a private treaty sale of a painting to the National Gallery.'[38] The Duke of Devonshire has raised at least £11 million from the sale of works of art to endow the charitable trust which owns a long term lease on Chatsworth, while a sale of Old Master drawings from the Chatsworth collection in 1984 realised £21 million for the Devonshire family.

The great majority of the new houses Robinson describes have been built by authentic landowners on traditional estates, 'including the inner circle of "Court" and "ruling" families like the Derbys, Halifaxes and Norfolks, and established eighteenth- and nineteenth-century dynasties like the Rothschilds, Hambros and Barings.'[39]

Financially, politically and culturally country houses and their owners appear to be more secure than we have been led to suppose.

It is no surprise to discover that few of these late twentieth-century houses have been built in a late twentieth-century style. A small group of architects have continued to build in versions of the Georgian architecture which is now considered the apogee of the country house manner. These have kept the rise of modernism at bay; latterly, it would appear that Georgian architecture is on the counter-attack.

The turning point was the completion of the new house of King's Walden Bury for Sir Thomas Pilkington in 1971. The architects were Raymond Erith and his former apprentice, Quinlan Terry. Erith, whose most celebrated commission had been the remodelling of 10, Downing Street, had been a classicist all his life, and made an appropriate master for Terry, who had rebelled against the modernist training imposed on him at the Architectural Association in the mid-1950s. He became Erith's partner in 1966, and together at King's Walden Bury they created an English evocation of the Italian villas of Palladio. They even used as module the Venetian fourteen-inch *piede* instead of the English twelve-inch foot. The building may have been conceived as the last country house – it became the first of a new generation.

Erith died in 1973, since when Quinlan Terry has become the dominant figure in what his supporters call simply 'the revival of architecture'. He built Waverton House for the banker Jocelyn Hambro in 1977, and Newfield House for the carpet manufacturer Michael Abrahams in 1979. He was originally employed by Sebastian de Ferranti to translate the romantic inventions of the painter Felix Kelly into a new version of Palladio's Villa Rotonda at Henbury Hall, Macclesfield, although his designs were rejected in favour of Julian Bicknall's. He has carried out small commissions for the National Trust, and in 1980 built a summerhouse for the then Secretary of State for the Environment Michael Heseltine. His classicism has not inhibited work for property developers. In 1982 Haslemere Estates employed him to redevelop Dufours Place, in Soho, as an eight-storey office block. The difference is that it is of traditional construction in load-bearing brick. This commission was followed by Haslemere's scheme for Richmond Riverside, a 109,000-feet square site which Terry has designed as not one office block, but fifteen separate buildings in a variety of classical styles.

Terry's commitment to classicism is more than aesthetic. He is a fundamentalist Christian and a warden at the church attended by Mrs

Mary Whitehouse. It is his personal belief that the orders of classical architecture are descended from the Temple of Solomon. As Clive Aslet has written in his study of Terry, the theory 'ingeniously unites the twin poles of his belief, Classicism and Christianity. . . . His belief in the God of order is reflected in an architecture of order, in which peace, harmony, quietness, rightness and simplicity are the dominant characteristics.'[40] But there is no doubt that the hierarchy of architectural orders is also a symbol of the hierarchy of social orders. Just as the right-wing aesthetician Roger Scruton has attacked modernism as 'the architecture of Leninism',[41] Aslet's study reveals the political agenda of classical revivalism. On the one hand, 'a building of 1790 – even a warehouse – is recognised as having an almost prelapsarian quality. It was built before architecture had lost its way.'[42] On the other, 'with or without due reason, belief in continuity has been considerably strengthened by the general elections of 1979 and 1983, and Terry is busy with more country houses than could have been predicted before Mrs Thatcher came to power.'[43]

Architecture is the most social of our art forms: Terry's function as a counter-revolutionary is summed up in Aslet's description of his work at Merks Hall, Essex, where he was consulted about work on a modern country house, built in 1961:

> The latter replied: 'It's not a gentleman's house.' This sealed its fate; it had to come down. But the 1961 house had in turn usurped the place of a Georgian house. As the walls of the present building rise triumphantly on their ridge about Great Dunmow in Essex – and Merks, with its belvedere, will be visible for miles around – there is a feeling in more than one way that the old order has been restored.[44]

Few of us can afford an architect of the skills of Quinlan Terry. Even Mrs Thatcher has had to content herself with the bastardised neo-Georgian of a Barratt House in Dulwich, and even then few of us could afford the £400,000 or more that she is reputed to have paid for it. Few of us can afford to live in the country, let alone a country house. We might, at a pinch, take up Wimpey's offer of renting a time-share apartment at Brantridge House in Somerset, 'one of the most beautiful and elegant private stately homes in the country', which formerly belonged to HRH Athlone, and we are assured, was 'a favourite Sussex retreat for the Royal Family'.[45]

Country house owners have had to adapt to more taxes and fewer servants, but like the Royal Family, they continue to serve as a social paradigm, and their values and tastes filter down, diluted for mass consumption. With the collapse of confidence during the 1970s, the country house has become a refuge even for those who are admitted only on an open day. As Peter York observed in 1984 'from the mid-Seventies a Grand Hotel or country house was the backdrop for every other fashion shot. And, of course, period Rehab was the mood in housing and construction.'[46] *The New Georgian Handbook* confirms 'Now that Modernism is dead, or at least, just another style, *houses are antiques for living in.*'[47]

The 'country house style' was largely the creation of John Fowler, co-founder of Colefax and Fowler, which continues to be one of the most prestigious interior design firms. He decorated most of the major houses in England, including the Queen's audience room at Buckingham Palace and carried out twenty four major projects for the National Trust, to whom he was principal adviser on decoration.

Fowler's country house style has since been popularised by Laura Ashley, a world-wide empire that has been built up since 1954 on the tasteful recreation of old fabric designs, rather than the production of new ones. Laura Ashley shops offer a complete costume both for houses and their female occupants. The 1985 catalogue, for instance, features, in succession, an English country house bedroom in a 'typically English late Victorian design of huge cabbage roses'; a Welsh country house breakfast room with a colour scheme 'whose origins lie in parochial English country houses of the 1820s'; a dining room in a small Georgian country house 'with a copy of eighteenth-century damask'; a garden pavilion for a chateau in Picardy, designed 'for a languid summer afternoon whiled away in the heart of the countryside' and so on through to a house in Provence; a Georgian house in Berkshire, and a nineteenth-century house on Long Island, New York.[48] A Laura Ashley catalogue sells its products by an appeal to the past and to the pleasures of the country house – the latest offers 'Charleston' fabrics that exploit the rescue and restoration of the farmhouse decorated by Vanessa Bell and Duncan Grant. Such are the movements of fashion, but one wonders what will be the consequences of Sir Roy Strong's declared intention to turn the Victoria and Albert Museum into 'the Laura Ashley of the 1990s'.

The new style of old values is steadily promoted by a rack of magazines, themselves founded to exploit the spread of retro-revivalism. *Country Life* now has a string of imitators, which are working on late twentieth-century variations of the combination of snobbery and rural nostalgia that launched it in 1897. The plush, urban environment of ruched curtains, ragged, dragged and marbled walls of *The World of Interiors* has its rural stablemate, *Country Homes and Interiors*, and its rival, *Traditional Interior Decoration*, together with *Traditional Homes*, which appeals to us to 'help preserve our architectural heritage' by buying the magazine, while our culinary heritage is cared

for by *Traditional Kitchens*. *Country Living* aims at the new, rather than the traditional, occupants of the countryside, and has the townsman's conservationist streak: Polly Devlin writes lyrically about the meadow she has preserved from modern farmers, a 'living museum that I and the likes of me guard in secret and count ourselves blessed to be able to do so.'[49] The overriding fantasy that we do not live in a built over world of town and suburbs is pressed home in *Out of Town, Britain's Countryside and Heritage Magazine*; this magical landscape, where it never rains except in paintings by Constable, is recruited to serve an idea of nationality in *Heritage: The British Review*. Both the Historic Houses association and the National Trust produce house journals which in style and format echo these commercial models.

As Quinlan Terry's fifteen variations on the classical rise beside the Thames at Richmond, it is possible to see such architecture taking over the present on behalf of the past. That it is able to do so is the result of a complex of issues that are only partly political: they have more to do with a deep cultural convulsion that manifests itself most clearly in our obsession with the past. This chapter has explored only aspects of this cultural nexus, but its themes draw together in a single, architectural emblem: the column designed by Quinlan Terry in 1975 and erected in the garden of a National Trust property, West Green House in Hampshire.

The house is leased to Lord McAlpine, a life peer created in 1984 and a director of the construction firm that has built many of Britain's office blocks. He is a collector and patron of the arts, and since 1975 has been Treasurer of the Conservative Party. The column was commissioned as part of McAlpine's plans for a 'philosophical garden', and in the case of the column, the philosophy is clear. Standing some forty feet high and placed deliberately near the public road, the column and finial of Portland stone bears a Latin inscription devised by Terry. In translation, it reads:

> This monument was built with a large sum of money, which
> would otherwise have fallen, sooner or later, into the hands
> of the tax-gatherers.[50]

Classicism seems the only appropriate mode in which to celebrate the campaign to defeat the wealth tax. Even the National Trust may feel some relief that Lord McAlpine's commission to erect a triumphal arch to celebrate the election of the first woman prime minister remains, as yet, unbuilt.

THE
INDUSTRIAL
DINOSAUR

VERY
FRAGILE

THE HERITAGE INDUSTRY

While the country houses offer dreams of Elysium, museums are smoothing away the nightmares of yesterday. An actress mourning by a coffin may do her best to evoke the hardships of working class life in 1900, but her performance is an entertainment that helps to make the past seem picturesque and pleasing. The country house becomes a stage upon which we can observe the lives of the upper classes: museums are turning into theatres for the re-enactment of the past.

The past is also getting closer. The opening of the Cabinet War Rooms in Whitehall has broken almost the last psychological barrier between yesterday and today. The chequered history of the Beatles Museum in Liverpool shows it is only just ahead of its time. With the country house secure, anxiety has transferred to a different sector of national memory – and national concern: our industrial past, and the simple objects of everyday life that evoke a time that has become remote, though it is well within living memory; only just the other side of the looking-glass.

The new vogue for historical re-enactments, not simply battles and sieges which license historicist hooliganism on Bank Holiday weekends, but the urge to recreate aspects of our former lives, from the Iron Age to the iron foundry, is evidence of the persistent fantasy that it is possible to step back into the past. Museums and fashion exploit the same nostalgic drive; the most contemporary attitude is a disdain for the present day.

Our political leaders collaborate in the blurring of today and yesterday, even at times becoming actors in the drama. When the Minister for the Arts, Richard Luce, visited the Yorkshire Museum in November 1986 to open a new display, 'How We Used to Live', an evocation of the period 1902 to 1926, he was happy to arrive in a 1920s Acomb taxi. He was also pleased to give his official blessing to York's growing museum culture. He visited the Railway Museum, and the latest word in museum presentation, the Jorvik Viking Centre, opened beneath a new shopping centre above an archeological site in 1984. Here Heritage Projects Ltd have installed the archeological equipment of the funfair ghost ride: a twelve-minute electric trolley tour round the recreation of a tenth-century village, peopled with dummies speaking twentieth-century Icelandic, but smelling 'authentically' of imagined Viking odours – livestock, foodstuffs, and a latrine.

These, Mr Luce observed, are part of a national and international 'museums explosion'. 'One of the most impressive facts in the art world today is the astonishing vitality of museums. Over the last fifteen years the number has doubled in the United Kingdom. There are about 2,000 of them – a great majority privately funded. Once every fortnight somewhere in the United Kingdom a new museum unfolds its treasures to the public gaze.'

Mr Luce recognised the social significance of these developments: they serve a function similar to that defined for the National Trust by its director general Angus Stirling: they are a source of reassurance and stability, or as Mr Luce puts it, the answer to 'an apparent human need for roots when all about us is changing so fast'. Museums are 'responding to a growing desire to learn about our past so we can face an ever more unpredictable future with greater confidence.'[1] But in York Mr Luce did not address himself to the reasons for the unpredictability of the future, or the reasons for the changes that drive us back on our roots. When museums become one of Britain's new growth industries, they are not signs of vitality, but symbols of national decline.

The statistic that the number of museums in Britain has doubled since 1960 is not in itself a symptom of decline, for a similar explosion has taken place elsewhere. Japan has opened 500 museums in fifteen years; both in Europe and North America every major city has been engaged in the creation of a new building or converting an old one. They are objects of pride and prestige; numbers are increasing because they create a focus for ideas of civic or national identity. In the twentieth century museums have taken over the function once exercised by church and ruler, they provide the symbols through which a nation and a culture understands itself. The great collections of Kings and Princes of the Church were displayed as treasure – the loot of plundered nations and expressions of personal wealth – and as propaganda – celebrations of the spiritual and political values of their owners. These functions did not disappear when crown and church lost their power to the more diffuse leadership of the modern state. One of the first actions of the new republicans of France after 1789 was to turn a royal palace into a national gallery, the Louvre.

The arrangement of museums and galleries, their selection and presentation, give the objects they contain a special significance. They serve the same functions as the selections that make written history. By displaying the evidence of past cultures, they help to locate a contemporary society in relation to a previous tradition. They give meaning to the present by interpreting the past. But this interpretative function does not stop there. As makers of meaning, they also interpret the present to itself. This explains the paradox that some of the most impressive new buildings of the late twentieth century – the Pompidou Centre in Paris, the new gallery in Los Angeles, the extension to the Staatsgalerie in Stuttgart – are museums of modern art.

Museums have become the new patrons of art. This has not only affected the shape of the art market, it has affected the nature of the art produced, which is conceived on the monumental scale of the institutions for which it is intended. Museum directors are high priests in the religion of culture, and often behave like them.

Museums sanction the creation of commodities that have immaterial, rather than material values. The objects that hold these values are a source of aesthetic pleasure, emotional response, historical knowledge, but above all, of cultural meaning. That is why although they are not displayed to be sold, and cannot in any way be possessed by the viewer, such objects are some of the most valuable a society can own. They represent a society's significance, and as such they are priceless. Not that these immaterial commodities do not also have an exchange value; people are prepared to pay to see them and support their acquisition, by attending museums in large numbers, and assenting to their support through taxation.

The cultural role that museums have inherited from the earlier institutions of crown and church explain the signficant difference between the state's attitude to funding museums and galleries, and to subsidy for the performing arts. The 'arm's length principle', which is intended to distance patronage of the arts from its political source, applies much less firmly in the world of museums and galleries, for although much of the growth in Britain in recent years has been in the independent sector, it is founded on a system of national and local museums which is rooted in the principle of direct political responsibility. It is significant that one of the most interesting and potentially influential collections of contemporary art has been formed by the Saatchi brothers, official image makers to Mrs Thatcher, and one of the largest advertising agencies in the world.

In the two-hundred-year history of museums, the function that has been ascribed to them has changed as radically as the interpretations that museums make; no more vividly than in Britain. With the exception of the Ashmolean Museum in Oxford, which opened its doors in 1683, the first major public museum in the world was the British Museum, founded by Act of Parliament in 1753. Like the Ashmolean, it was created from earlier private collections, but, as its title and inception suggest, it was intended as a national, secular institution, with an educational purpose. Originally it housed history, art and science, but as the collections grew they also divided, so that the creation of the National Gallery followed in 1824, the National Portrait Gallery in 1856, and the Tate Gallery in 1896. The science collections moved to South Kensington in 1883. This process continues, for the British Library only gained separate status in 1974, and will move into a new building in the 1990s. Access to the British Museum was always intended to be free of charge, though other restrictions on visitors to the galleries were not entirely lifted until 1879, by which time the collections were housed in the present British Museum building, begun in 1823.

The creation of such a national institution was an example to local pride. Whereas in 1800 there had been fewer than a dozen public museums in Britain, by 1850 there were nearly sixty. The earliest were the creation of local learned societies following the educational model of the British Museum, but while the educational intention was never lost, museums began to take on a new social and economic function. In the burgeoning cities of the industrial north, museums and libraries began to be founded as a distraction and a refreshment for the working population. They were to raise the moral and educational tone of cities – and counteract drunkenness and fornication. The principle of public funding was extended by the Museum Act of 1845, which empowered borough councils with a population of more than 10,000 to levy a halfpenny rate to establish a public museum of art and science; libraries were added in 1850 and legislation extended by further Museums Acts.

In addition to the moral purpose there was an economic one: the improvement of knowledge of design, with a view to the improvement of manufacturing skills. As early as 1836 the government had founded a school of design, in order to strengthen the quality of British design in the face of foreign competition. The Great Exhibition of 1851 was an extension of the same policy, and from it came a Museum of Manufactures, established at Marlborough House in London. This in turn organised touring exhibitions which served to stimulate the foundation of local museums. Much of the responsibility for the spread of museums in the latter half of the nineteenth century was that of Henry Cole, the chief organiser of the Great Exhibition, who subsequently ran the education department of the Board of Trade. Cole controlled both the increasing number of government design schools and the Museum of Manufactures. In 1857 the museum moved to South Kensington, and in 1899, when the Science Museum became a separate entity, this much expanded collection was renamed the Victoria and Albert Museum.

Between 1850 and 1914 nearly 300 museums were founded in provincial towns and cities, and were supported by local authorities through the rates. By 1939 there were 400 local authority museums. In theory, the museum system in the United Kingdom consists of a top tier of twenty-four museums of 'national status'; a nationwide network of local authority museums, some sixteen museums and galleries maintained by universities, a group of military museums based on the collections of individual regiments and services, and finally the independent sector, where museums vary in size and source of funding: some are commercial ventures, but the majority are the responsibility of non-profit-distributing charitable trusts. In practice, the distribution and funding of museums is more haphazard. The Office of Arts and Libraries, which is responsible for museum policy, funds only eleven of the national museums; eight different ministries fund the rest.

The distribution and quality of local authority museums varies considerably. *Museums UK* points out that 'although there are currently no counties in the United Kingdom without some form of museum provision, in real terms this spatial distribution is markedly uneven with a strong tendency for concentration within the south of England.'[2] It should be noted that this 'North/South divide' also applies to the conservation movement generally. Sixty per cent of local amenity societies are in the south, six southern counties have over two-thirds of the listed buildings. The *English Heritage Monitor, 1977* pointed out that 'National Trust membership is also biased toward the south and is known to be largely middle-class and middle-aged', adding 'National Trust and private properties to tend to be found in rural locations in the south of England.'[3]

A significant recent development has been the granting of a Royal Charter to the Museums and Galleries Commission on 1 January 1987. First set up in 1931 as a purely advisory body, the Commission has grown in authority and influence, and is now attempting to regulate the disordered museum world. While it advises the government on museum policy, and has taken over responsibility for the administration of the acceptance of objects (but not land or buildings) in lieu of tax, it is not concerned with the national museums, which are mainly governed by independent trustees. But in England it funds the seven Area Museums Councils which represent the interests of both local authority and independent museums. Out of a total grant from the government of £6 million, it assists non-national museums with purchase grants and a limited amount of capital spending, while the Area Museums Councils distribute funds in their respective areas on its behalf. The Commission insists that it has no interest in managing or directly funding museums, but the decision to start a system for the registration of museums, which will impose minimum standards for any institution seeking public funding will have an important regulatory effect. Backed by its Royal Charter and with the economic authority of government funding behind it, the Commission will be in a position to decide what a museum is. By defining its standards, it will be defining its meaning.

The question of definition is important, for the doubling of the number of museums since 1960 has been the result of the growth in the independent sector. Of museums founded since 1950 – and particularly since 1971 – fifty-six per cent have been in the private sector, and the number continues to expand.

The prospect of Britain becoming 'one big open air museum' is less comic than it might at first appear. The phenomenal rise in the number of museums reflects not only a new interest in museums as a source of cultural meaning, but the development of a new kind of museum, with a new function. Many of the new museums are devoted to the recent past and the everyday – 'The Way We Were' at Wigan Pier, 'How We Used to Live' at York, the new open air museums. The urge is to recall not military greatness or the emergence of the nation state, but Victorian Britain, or even more poignantly, the 1920s and 1930s. Now, nostalgia is for the industrial past. For Dr Cossons of the Science Museum this raises some difficult questions about the present:

It reflects the huge rate of de-industrialisation and the change which that has brought about in the last ten or fifteen years. We want something to hang on to, I suppose. We can't continue because we can't afford all the museums we have probably got now. The paradox is that the first generation of museums were afforded by a booming industrial Victorian society, here we are in the process of becoming poor and post-industrial (if you take the gloomy view, which I don't) and we can't afford to look after the remnants of that industrial revolution, which is the whole of the Victorian heritage which represents something like seventy per cent of our built environment.[4]

Dr Cossons is a former director of one of the independent museums which have pioneered the preservation of industrial history, the Ironbridge Gorge Museum in Shropshire. The rise of industrial archeology is an ironic commentary on the decline of the industries it studies.

As recently as 1972 it was possible for an industrial archeologist, Dr Robert Buchanan, to write of his subject having in the future 'possibly, the status of an academic discipline'.[5] The remains of previous stages of industrialisation only became interesting when they were threatened by post-war modernisation, in the shape of industrial reconstruction, urban renewal and the building of motorways. The Council for British Archeology appointed a research committee for industrial archeology in 1960. The first major industrial conservation battle was fought – and lost – in 1962, around the elegant neo-classical arch at the entrance to Euston Station. The arch was of architectural as well as railway interest, but Euston station was redeveloped just the same. The Council for British Archeology began a survey of industrial monuments, and set up an advisory panel to recommend on what should and should not be preserved. In 1965 a report from the Ancient Monuments Board called for an agreed policy on preserving significant structures. Following a passionate conference on industrial archeology in London in 1969, the *Economist* commented 'industrial archeology is just ceasing to be regarded as a hobby for harmless lunatics.'[6]

The Association for Industrial Archeology was founded in 1973, the year of the oil crisis, and the real growth in the subject has been since then. This growth should be set against Britain's decline as an industrial nation. In 1913 Britain produced 30.2 per cent of the world's exported manufactures, in 1958 29.3 per cent, in 1960 16.5 per cent, in 1970 10.6 per cent and in 1985 7.9 per cent. Ironically, part of the inefficiency of British industry is due to the age of the buildings: forty per cent of factory floorspace is pre-1945, nearly twenty per cent pre-1914. We have ceased to be a net exporter of manufactures, and in 1987 faced a deficit of £8,000 million in manufactured goods. While the industrial base upon which the British economy has traditionally rested has been shrinking, it has also been declining as a source of employment, and fell dramatically after 1970. It is the steady de-industrialisation of Britain which has done so much to create the climate of decline, particularly in the north of England, where unemployment is highest and the evidence of decline in terms of closed factories and derelict buildings most visible. Excluding the

self-employed, ninety-four per cent of the job losses between 1979 and 1986 were in the Midlands and the North. The House of Lords Select Committee on Industry whose 1985 report warned that this decline threatens our economic and political stability, heard evidence that as much as a sixth of Britain's manufacturing capability has been scrapped and not replaced during the 1980s.

While the real world of industrial manufacturing decays, redundant and obsolete machinery flourishes – in museums. Within a hundred years we have begun to conserve and protect some of the very things, such as railway lines and factories, which sparked off the urge to rediscover and protect the Britain that the National Trust for Places of Historic Interest or Natural Beauty believed was threatened. Now that time has eroded their function, industrial monuments, defined as 'any relic of an obsolete phase of an industry or transport system, ranging from a Neolithic flint mine to a newly obsolete aircraft or electronic computer'[7], can be accommodated into the safe and pleasing past.

Anthony Burton's *Remains of a Revolution* was published in 1975 to demonstrate how recent the study of industrial history was, but the text and photographs describe a world that has been absorbed by the picturesque aesthetic. Burton intended 'to give an idea of the often surprising beauty to be found in early industrial architecture and of the delight to be discovered in seeing machines at work, performing tasks for which they were designed two centuries ago.'[8]

The National Trust entered the world of industrial archeology in 1960, when it accepted responsibility for the restoration of twenty-six and a half miles of the Stratford upon Avon Canal, and it first appointed an industrial adviser in 1964. It has since acquired four Cornish beam engines and the Conway suspension bridge, but has felt it should take second place to independent industrial archeology groups. It had acquired a cotton mill and its associated village at Styal in Cheshire in 1939, but the factory did not come into the Trust's control until 1959. (In the 1950s government grants were used to pay for the destruction of obsolete machinery.) The Trust maintains its interest in the village, but has passed the management of the Quarry Bank Mill to an industrial trust, which has set the surviving machinery in motion once again. There are now 464 museums possessing collections of industrial material, of which a third are museums founded since 1970, and 817 museums with collections relating to rural history, the majority founded since 1960.[9]

Ironbridge Gorge Museum has set the pace. At its heart is the cast-iron bridge built over the River Severn in 1779 by a local ironmaster, Abraham Darby, but the museum is spread over seven separate sites along the narrow valley where the conjunction of iron ore, coal and

river created the conditions for the first stages of the industrial revolution. In 1959 the site of Abraham Darby's foundry at Coalbrookdale was opened as a museum by the firm that continued to work on the site, but much of the industry in the valley was derelict. In 1966 the idea of turning the whole area into a museum was being actively canvassed, but it was the decision in 1968 to designate an area to the north of the valley as Telford New Town that brought the museum into being. The Ironbridge Gorge Museum Trust was formed with the deliberate intention of providing the new town with a sense of identity that drew on the area's long association with iron and steel.

Ironically, while the British steel industry has gone the way of the Coalbrookdale Iron Works, the Severn Gorge is one of the more prosperous sections of Telford New Town, with shops and hotels, and the once derelict houses selling at premium prices. The ruin of Abraham Darby's foundry is protected by a housing of metal and glass: the cradle of the industrial revolution is also its reliquary, treated with the reverence of a shrine.

The Ironbridge Gorge Museum does have a basis in historical fact, in that it has been built round the ruins that are its exhibits, though the reconstructed industrial village at Blist's Hill has all the authenticity of a film set. But its contemporary, Beamish Open Air Museum, just south of Newcastle upon Tyne has a more ironic relationship to the region whose life it memorialises. Beamish is funded by a consortium of local authorities in the North East, an area whose prosperity was built on coal, steel and ship building, but which has suffered most severely from the recession. Yet before the museum opened in 1970, the only connection the site had with industry was that Beamish Hall and its surrounding estate had previously been owned by the National Coal Board.

Beamish is an attempt to reconstruct the life of the North East on a green field site. The 200 acres of farmland and wood are dotted with the materials of the region's past: a railway station, a town street, a row of miners' cottages, a colliery, all neatly linked by a tramline as if it were the layout for a model railway. The buildings are genuine enough, but they have all come from somewhere else. The Georgian terrace comes from Gateshead, the miners' cottages stood in Hetton-Le-Hole until 1976, the Co-Op shop comes from Anfield Plain. Each building is carefully refurnished as well as rebuilt, and although Beamish does not as yet employ actors, the attendants are in costume and know the scenario that has been provided for each house.

The height of historic invention is achieved at the Beamish colliery. It is true that there was coal on the site – the bulk of it removed from what is now the car park by open cast mining once the museum was

under construction – and the re-opened primitive drift mine is genuine, but the workings for the deep mine stand over a shaft that is not there. The winding engine house is original – but it was controversially moved half a mile from the pit it once served to its present position, and instead of steam an electric motor now turns its wheels. By the non-existent pit shaft stands the pit heap: what elsewhere would be considered an eyesore is here a lovingly reconstructed fake.

The paradox of Beamish is not that it is false, the exhibits are as genuine as they could possibly be, but that it is more real than the reality it seeks to recall. The town street evokes an indistinct period of between the two wars, at just that distance in time when memory softens and sweetens. But there is no need for personal nostalgia. Here, the displays do it for you. The effect is so complete that it is the late twentieth-century visitors, not the buildings, that seem out of place. Beamish only looks 'right' when it is taken over by one of the television companies that regularly use it as a location.

Yet while this charming world was being created, the life of the North East was being destroyed. Many of the thousands of items that the museum's first director Frank Atkinson was gathering and storing in the decade before the site was found came to him because of redevelopment and dispersal as the old communities were breaking up. And amidst all this it seems that there are still some industrial monuments which we would prefer not to preserve.

Ten miles from Beamish is the town of Consett. Like Ironbridge, Consett has a long industrial history, and from the 1840s was dominated by its steel works. In 1980 the British Steel Corporation closed the works down, with the loss of 3,500 jobs, and many more jobs went with the removal of the town's economic *raison d'être*. Adult unemployment is around twenty-five per cent, and youth unemployment eighty per cent. New firms have been enticed to the area, but Consett's largest new employer is Derwent Valley Foods, where 110 people are engaged in the production of snacks packaged under the pseudo-nineteenth-century patronage of Phileas Fogg. The site of the steelworks has been razed, in spite of the appeal from Beamish that one furnace should be preserved: as a tourist attraction. In Consett, such a relic would have a different meaning, as a monument not to industrial enterprise, but as a reminder of the near death of a town through de-industrialisation.

The collapse of the manufacturing economy of the North East has meant that the significance of Beamish has also changed. It is no longer an educational resource or the repository of memory: it is an employer, and an economic asset as a tourist attraction. As industries die, the heritage solution is increasingly applied. There is now a plan to turn the defunct Hawthorn Leslie shipyard in Hebburn, south of the Tyne,

into a national shipbuilding centre. New ships are not being built any more, but there are two separate schemes to build replica Victorian clippers, one on the Wear, one on the Tyne. In the West Midlands, where the number of engineering firms has fallen from 1,400 in 1978 to 950 in 1985, and at least 235,000 engineering jobs have disappeared, the Black Country Museum, a clone of Beamish, is being promoted as a tourist attraction.

In Wales redundant miners bought the Big Pit colliery in Gwent for £1 when the Coal Board closed it down in 1980, and then re-opened it as a museum. In the Rhondda Valley, where male unemployment is thirty-three per cent, 800 jobs were lost when the Lewis Merthyr colliery was shut down in 1983. Now there is a plan to offer 'a total mining experience', and ex-miners will re-enact their redundant roles in a newly built mining village that will produce coal only for tourists. A local authority official explains: 'Unless we have a heritage concept now, in five year's time we won't be able to link the Rhondda with its illustrious past.'[10]

The measures become more desperate and fantastical. The site of another Rhondda colliery has become a Wild West adventure play-ground for grown ups. In the steel town of Corby in Northamptonshire, where the works closed in 1980, they are still waiting for the wonder-world theme park that is supposed to be built on a thousand acres of old iron ore diggings. Back in Northumbria, South Tyneside has become, according to the road signs, 'Catherine Cookson Country'. The prolific writer of historical romances was born in South Shields, and lent her name to the promotion launched in 1985 by South Tyneside Council. The fact that the houses where she was born and brought up, in, by all accounts, miserable circumstances, were demolished long ago was no obstacle to the invention of a tourist trail. A replica street has been built in the South Shields Museum, and a Catherine Cookson Museum is on the drawing board.

Such desperate measures are not only the product of economic neces-sity: there is also a need to create a past that will substitute for the erasures of the present. But the accuracy of the 'everyday life' depicted in museums like Beamish is rarely questioned, nor is the motivation of the conservation movement, which seeks to apply a museum solution to the whole fabric of the environment. Yet as P. A. Faulkner, Superintending Architect in the Ancient Monuments and Historic Buildings Division of the Department of the Environment, argued in a Royal Society of Arts lecture in 1978, 'very often the image we have of the past is by no means based on reality.'

97

Perhaps this is nowhere more apparent than in the conservation of the urban or village scene. It is undoubtedly desirable that we should preserve the typical English village. It represents a way of life that is unquestionably part of our historic heritage. But, are we really clear what we mean by this? And of what period are we talking? Most of us have in our minds some sort of Candleford-like self-sufficient community, with only primitive communications, but this no longer exists nor can it exist in today's society. It has since acquired tarmacadam roads, telephone wires, a substation, power lines and so on.[11]

Quoting as an example the changes made to the village of Alcester, which in 1975 won a Heritage Year Award from the Civic Trust, Faulkner argued that, with modernising elements adjusted or removed, 'We have created the village we should like to see; not preserved that which was in fact there.'[12]

Faulkner is driven to the conclusion that if we are to adopt policies for conservation then we will have to apply our arguments with greater intellectual rigour. 'In speaking of the built environment conservation and preservation have acquired a different meaning, the latter having little to do with the former, whatever the dictionary might say.'[13]

If we truly wish to preserve the memorials of the past, then the distinction between conservation and preservation becomes downright conflict. Preservation means the maintenance of an object or building, or such of it as remains, in a condition defined by its historic context, and in such a form that it can be studied with a view to revealing its original meaning. Conservation, on the other hand, creates a new context and, if only by attracting the attention of members of the public, a new use. Professor Peter Fowler of Newcastle University, a former chairman of the Royal Commission on Ancient Monuments, has consistently argued that the display of archaeological discoveries 'usually in fact means damage and sometimes destruction. Subsequent care and maintenance where this has happened could well be of a modern piece of quasi-heritage, impressive maybe for the public but a monumental dodo from an academic point of view.'[14] If we really are interested in our history, then we may have to preserve it from the conservationists.

Display is not even an answer to the financial problems of the building it is meant to preserve. As the SAVE Britain's Heritage 1982 pamphlet *Preserve and Prosper* makes clear: 'Tourism by itself will not provide all the funds necessary for preserving old buildings. Indeed the costs of tourism, in the form of the payment of staff for guiding, security, extra facilities, and wear-and-tear, will sometimes exceed the revenue from visitors.'[15] This is born out by the case of Ely Cathedral, which spends £262,375 out of an annual maintenance budget of £515,231 to meet the needs of visitors. The revenue they generated was £237,017, which means that each visitor to Ely cost the cathedral on average a net loss of twelve pence.[16]

Yet if the buildings themselves do not profit from tourism, other aspects of the economy do. SAVE's pamphlet continues: 'The main economic benefit will be derived by transport, accommodation, catering and retailing businesses. In this context the historic building is a classical example of the "loss leader".'[17] As on Tyneside, as in the Rhondda Valley, the past is no longer a finite entity but a resource, sometimes the last resource. As such it is shaped and moulded to the needs of the present, and in the process filtered, polished and drained of meaning. Yet the substitution of this imaginary past has become official policy, even as the same government elsewhere has allowed the present to decline.

The test bed for this policy has been Liverpool, the first nineteenth-century city to be made redundant by the twentieth. The collapse of the transatlantic shipping trade in the 1960s and the failure of manufacturing industries in the face of recession has meant that the city has lost one-third of its population. Those that remain face an average unemployment rate of eighteen per cent, but far worse in the black and Asian quarters. In Toxteth sixty per cent of young blacks are out of work. Resentment and disaffection has been rife, and in 1981 the rancour turned to rioting. The problems of Liverpool and other cities had already been recognised by the 1974 Labour government's creation of Inner City Partnerships to co-ordinate the use of central funds in areas of exceptional need, but as the former Conservative Minister for the Environment, Michael Heseltine, has written: 'It is widely agreed that the jolt given by the urban riots of the 1980s provided the motive power' to seek to revive such blighted areas.[18] In 1982 the Merseyside Development Corporation was set up with sweeping planning and financial powers.

The role of Michael Heseltine is important, not only because he associated himself so strongly with Liverpool, but because of the policies he brought to the questions of environment and urban renewal. His attempt to bring industrial investment to Liverpool by bussing thirty captains of industry round the city's worst areas taught him that there had to be something more than the challenge to attract business back. The Liverpool Garden Festival was called into being: 'Stoke-on-Trent was the rival candidate, but before we had made our choice the Toxeth riots occurred, and it seemed to me urgent to dispel the sudden sense of failure and loss by starting something in central

Liverpool that was new and would succeed.'[19] The answer to the lack of jobs appeared to be trees. The cleaning up of Liverpool was not without its ironies. During the riots the Racquets Club in Upper Parliament Street, once the resort of slave owning merchants, was burnt to the ground. A one hundred per cent Derelict Land Grant from the Department of the Environment enabled the Rural Preservation Association to turn the site into a wildlife refuge.

The Liverpool Garden Festival of 1984, which cost the Development Corporation £11 million to reclaim the land and £19 million to install, could only have at best a cosmetic effect, and it has not been possible to find a tenant to take over the site. The Albert Docks represent a long-term attempt at regeneration through musuems. In the 1960s these splendid but technologically redundant Victorian buildings faced demolition for redevelopment. In 1969 the City Planning Officer said: 'It is unreal to expect local interests, in an area which has suffered for many decades from chronic unemployment, to consider the preservation of a building to be more important than the opportunity of 40,000 jobs.'[20] In 1971 even that possibility disappeared when the developers withdrew. The Mersey Docks and Harbour Company abandoned the buildings which, in spite of a Grade I listing, were left to decay.

In 1984 the Albert Docks began a new life – as a museum, in fact a series of museums, for while one wing houses the new Merseyside Maritime Museum, another wing is being prepared for the Tate Gallery of the North. The now abolished Merseyside County Council had launched a pilot scheme for a Maritime Museum on a site next to the Albert Docks in 1979. When the Development Corporation was set up in 1982 it immediately agreed to house the museum within the docks, and set about a £2.25 million refurbishment of Block D. The Tate Gallery of the North will cost £2 million, and a further £9.25 million has been spent on civil engineering, including new lock gates, and landscaping the site. Out of the ten museums recommended for promotion by a House of Commons enquiry in 1982 the Merseyside museums, of which the maritime collection is part, are the only ones to have been awarded national status, and thus direct government funding. The motive is economic and political. The abolition of Merseyside County Council in 1986 left the region with museums bigger than the local authorities that inherited its responsibilities were able to support, while the decay of the area demanded national intervention.

The Urban Development Grant scheme established in 1982 as a result of the Heseltine Merseyside 'taskforce' experiment encourages local authorities to prepare schemes in cooperation with local capital in order to bid for central government funds which will cover three quarters of the local authority commitment. Conservation qualifies for urban aid, thus the refurbishment of the Adelphi Hotel in Liverpool secured a grant of £1.4 million. The cultural investment in the Albert Docks is not ultimately directed at the museums, but to support the further £16 million pumped into the restaurants, shops and offices that are also being developed there, and at the tourists who, it is hoped, will come. To provide for their entertainment, the Merseyside Development Corporation has an annual community budget of £100,000, contributing for instance £10,000 to a Festival of Comedy, and £7,500 to a show of sculpture.

While further Development Corporations are being established in Cardiff, Manchester, the Black Country, Tyneside and Teeside, the logic of the museum strategy in Liverpool has been applied to the whole of the government's historic estate. Under Michael Heseltine the Department of the Environment prepared to 'privatise' its responsibility for ancient monuments, castles and other buildings under its control by establishing the Historic Buildings and Monuments Commission for England. The commission also took over the Ministry's job of scheduling and listing monuments, buildings and gardens, grant aid to churches, the works of the Historic Buildings Council for England, maintaining a national archeological service and funding rescue archeology. Established by the National Heritage Act, 1983, and governed by independent commissioners chaired by Lord Montagu of Beaulieu, the organisation operates under the title English Heritage, to the annoyance of the National Heritage Memorial Fund, which feels it has a prior claim to the word under its own National Heritage Act of 1980.

Although its funds come entirely from the government – £63 million in 1987/88 – English Heritage, as far as the 400 properties in its care are concerned, is adopting the model of the National Trust, by promoting a membership scheme that has already attracted more than 45,000 people. Under Lord Montagu, author of *How to live in a Stately Home and Make Money*[21], English Heritage has set out aggresively to market the properties for which it is responsible to the public. Its line now is 'Visit an English Heritage property and enjoy a range of spectacular entertainment.'[22] Sponsored by Gateway Foodmarkets, more than forty military and historical displays have been staged in 1987, from Roman army drill to training for World War One. The participants in such events pride themselves on the accuracy of their manoeuvres and accoutrements. And see nothing absurd in restaging the American War of Independence on English soil.

While English Heritage moves into the tourist business, the English Tourist Board has become a major investor in museums. Capital grants from the English Tourist Board have been a significant factor in the growth of independent museums. In 1986/87 a total of £370,000 was spent on some nineteen different projects. In 1986 £84.4 million worth of capital projects involving cultural and historical schemes were in hand. This too is government money, provided under the Development of Tourism Act of 1969. The government's grant in aid to the English Tourist Board rose to £11.3 million for 1987/88, and the Tourism Development Fund was increased by twenty eight per cent to £12 million. Significantly, the Ministry sponsoring tourism changed in 1985 from the Department of Trade and Industry to the Department of Employment.

If the first report by the all-party House of Commons Environment Committee (1987) is anything to go by, the interests of tourism will become even more dominant in government policies on conservation. The recommendation that attracted most attention was that cathedrals should charge every visitor £1 for, in spite of the 'wear and tear' of tourism, the report saw this as the best means of ensuring the buildings' survival, at least until sufficient public funds were made available. Astonishingly, English Heritage was criticised for putting too little emphasis on tourism, and was 'unequivocally' urged to do more. The patriotic argument for tourism shifted effortlessly into the defence of self-help:

> This is because not only must we be ready and proud to share this precious heritage with the rest of the world but also because the more people who experience it, the more will be ready to see it is protected and conserved. The most direct and effective way in which, in the present economic climate, English Heritage can promote the conservation of England's historic buildings and ancient monuments is by promoting tourist interest in them. Ultimately, this would be of far more effect than a lament at the shortage of public funds.[23]

The heritage industry has become a vital part of the economic underpinning of the country. It is not for nothing that the English Tourist Board publishes an annual *English Heritage Monitor*. It is a godsend to the Manpower Services Commission, which is charged with mopping up the army of unemployed. The MSC Community Programme creates jobs that otherwise would not have existed, such as weaving, grinding corn and living in a reconstruction of an Iron Age round house at Manchester Museum. In 1985 214 museums ran MSC schemes, producing the equivalent of 2,206 full-time jobs, and a further 2,000 were employed in archeology. Independent museums rely heavily on MSC workers. The Museums Association's *Museums*

UK points out that many museums are now dependent on volunteers and the MSC 'to carry out even their most basic museum functions.'[24] In 1986 the National Trust was able to use 3,800 people in 300 different schemes, mainly estate work, worth £11 million. But industrial museums are no substitute for industrial enterprises, nor are Community Programme jobs real jobs. Beamish Open Air Museum trains the drivers of redundant 1920s trams, but at the end of twelve months, it is the man, not the tram, that goes.

The economic justification for conservation schemes is often the result of weakness: there is nothing else that can be done with the building except turn it into a museum; there is nothing else to be done with the people except temporarily to employ them as museum attendents. When the heritage argument meets real financial forces it crumbles. In 1985 the City of London drew up a draft plan to become a 'Heritage City', and preserve such of its character as remained. This attitude had helped to defeat the scheme to build a Mies van der Rohe office block at the Mansion House in 1984. (The developer, Peter Palumbo, preferred the services of the neo-Georgian Architect Claud Phillimore when it came to his private house.) But when it became clear that the expansionist demands of the Big Bang meant that the financial houses might go outside the City to less conservation-minded neighbouring local authorities, or to the planning free-for-all of London Docklands, the City plan was abandoned. The ecological movement has found itself impotent in the face of the drive to build a Channel tunnel.

The paradox of the industrial museum movement is that it is ultimately anti-industrial, as the director of the Science Museum, Dr Cossons, recognises:

> There is an anti-industrial, anti-technological feeling which has grown up enormously in the last twenty to twenty-five years. And the – sort of scratch an Englishman and you find a Morris Dancer sort of thing, you know. We're an industrial nation desperately pretending not to be. And it is quite remarkable, it seems to me, how many people do not want to have anything to do with the wealth-generating process that we call industry. Industry has got a very bad press, it is associated in the minds of so many people now, with all sorts of decline in economic terms. But it is still what we are going to survive on.[25]

The heritage movement may have been recruited to serve the interests of economic regeneration, but its ideology can also prove an obstacle. The National Coal Board – renamed British Coal – has plans to remove the largest slag heap in Britain, 114 acres at Cutacre Clough in Lancashire, in order to dig an open cast mine that will produce 850,000 tonnes of industrial coal, £130 million for the Board, 150 jobs, and not destroy agricultural land. But British Coal has been challenged by local environmentalists who wish to preserve the heap, and they appear to have the local authorities on their side. George Orwell's civilization founded on coal has acquired a completely different meaning.

V

THE POLITICS OF PATRONAGE

One of the justifications offered for the efforts of the heritage industry is that today has a responsibility to yesterday: to preserve it so that it may be handed on to tomorrow. Yet if the associations of heritage with inheritance are to be taken seriously, then our contemporary culture should have something to add to this patrimony. It is doubtful that in the face of a growing obsession with the past that the contemporary arts will have much room to make such a contribution. It is a sign of the times that government's spending on museums and galleries has been increasing faster than on the live arts. Some people may even welcome this: art that is still being made is less easily assimilated into the closed frame of heritage culture, with its air of permanence and completion. Such work may indeed call into question the cultural values that the heritage industry reinforces. If so, it is unlikely to be permitted to flourish within the official system of cultural patronage.

'The arts are to British tourism what the sun is to Spain', declared the chairman of the Arts Council of Great Britain Sir William Rees-Mogg in a lecture in March 1985, adding, with a touch of *lèse-majesté*, 'of course we must not forget the heritage and the monarchy which, with the arts, support a tourist trade which brings in some £5,000 million.'[1] Thus the whole of British culture, from the pomp and circumstance of the Crown to *No Sex Please, We're British*, is reduced to a statistic by the head of the organisation instituted to foster the imagination and creative spirit of a nation. The arts are the servants of development corporations now. 'As British manufacturing declines, there must be investment in the expansion of invisible earnings; and the arts are an essential part of any rational policy for such investment.'[2]

Sir William should not be blamed for recognising an economic reality: what is significant is the way that the Arts Council has actively embraced and reinforced the conditions which he describes. The economic role of culture was similarly recognised in the report of a House of Commons select committee in 1982, which accepted without question that 'the arts are a major industry in their own right. We estimate that the arts directly employ not less than 200,000 people, and that the turnover of the arts industry in 1981–82 approached £900 million.'[3] This excluded books and libraries; if broadcasting, publishing and ancillary industries (but not the Royal Family) were included, the figure would be more than £3,000 million.

The Arts Council contributes only a fraction of this sum. According to Sir William the Arts Council's grant of £100 million for 1985 financed some £250 million in turnover.[4] The BBC, commercial television, the record industry, publishing and such of the film industry that survives are all important contributors to the total. But the Arts Council has a central role in defining the terms and setting the conditions in which any discussion of the arts can take place. Like museums, the Arts Council helps to establish cultural meanings, and like museums its own context and purpose has changed. During the 1980s it has been at the centre of a debate about the nature and appropriate forms of patronage for the arts. It is not accidental that Sir William should call his lecture 'The Political Economy of Art'.

Until the 1980s the common consensus in Britain – though not in Continental Europe, where ministerial direction of subsidy is a matter of course – was that the arts had to be kept at some distance from political control. By 'the arts' are meant the performing arts and the work of contemporary visual artists and writers. As the last chapter argued, the conservation and presentation of art works of the past were from the beginning the subject of direct political patronage. Thus in Britain the two opposite forms of public spending on the arts – direct and indirect – have existed side by side.

It should be understood, however, that both are forms of state patronage. As Sir William says, 'the Arts Council is the state's instrument for helping the living arts.'[5] It exists to exercise the state's power at arm's length. The justification for the apparent surrender of direct government control – and the same principle applies to the covey of quangos that includes English Heritage and the Museums and Galleries Commission – is that the organisations which stand in for the state drain subsidy of party political colouring. As the doyen of the cultural aristocracy of the old school, Lord Goodman, chairman of the Arts Council from 1965 to 1972, said in 1984, 'our system has, up to now, insulated the arts against political interference.'[6]

Lord Goodman's lawyer's caution in the phrase 'up to now' suggests that the system has been changing, but the real question is to what extent the system can ever be truly free from political interference, not only in individual decisions, but in the existence of the Arts Council as a political creation.

The Arts Council came into being in 1945, as part of the post-war Welfare State. Its origins were propagandist, in that it grew out of the Council for the Encouragement of Music and Arts, whose foundation in 1940 set the precedent for state funding of the performing and contemporary arts. Its funds come directly from government, but the responsible minister is supposed to have no direct say in their application, nor, for that matter, does he have to answer for the Arts Council in Parliament. The power of the government is limited to the size of the annual grant, financial scrutiny, and the appointment of the chairman and nineteen other people who constitute the governing council.

These unpaid public figures in turn appoint a professional secretariat, and can call upon the advice of more volunteers who, under the chairmanship of council members, make up the advisory panels which consider the distribution of funds among the various art forms. The members of the advisory panels usually have some professional expertise, but few of the twenty members of the Arts Council, perhaps half a dozen at any one time, could be described as artists. The rest represent the customary quango mix of businessmen, regional politicians, academics, the occasional trade unionist and other 'cultured generalists' from the Great and the Good, which garrison such outposts of government. As we saw earlier, it is common to serve on more than one such organisation at a time, and there is free movement between them, both at board and professional level. Lord Gibson, chairman of the Arts Council from 1972 to 1977 subsequently became chairman of the National Trust. Angus Stirling, who had served under him at the Arts Council, became director-general of the Trust during Gibson's period of office.

Far from removing an element of political interference from the arts, the Arts Council merely diffuses it. It is a compromise between the traditional form of state and aristocratic patronage, and the bureaucratic patronage of professional groups. In both cases, their interests are represented on, and catered for by, the Arts Council. But while appearing to block direct political interference from above, the system also blocks it from below. The Council regularly makes the point that council members, and more especially those who advise on policy in specific areas, are not 'representative' of any particular organisation. Clearly, they must have a specialist knowledge of some kind to qualify as decision makers, but experience and a specific interest in any issue have somehow to be separated in the adviser or council member's mind. This difficult concept was explained to the House of Commons Select Committee on the Arts in 1982 by the then chairman of the Arts Council, Kenneth Robinson:

> The great virtue of the Council as a collection of individuals
> is that no one has any vested interests at all. They are people
> appointed because of their interests in the arts, either a

particular art or more than one art or the arts generally, and they have no motivation whatever other than to try and reach decisions which are in the best interests of the furtherance of the arts collectively in this country. I think the moment you have representatives who may be mandated to take a particular point of view, this objectivity goes out of the window.[7]

The assumption of objectivity is highly questionable. Without subjective knowledge a member would be useless to the Council. What Robinson really means is that the particular vested interests of Council members are so close to the interests of the Council that they magically become objective. The specific tastes of a caste or profession are generalised into the tastes of the organisation whose judgements define the official parameters of art.

The Council is able to follow its own principles of 'quality' and 'standards' without having to define what they are. Instead of conducting an open debate, they are free to work with a number of assumed generalities which in practice have the effect that 'quality' simply means that which the Arts Council chooses to support. The operation of consensus, which leads to generalities that rely heavily on the concept of tradition, has an in-built inertia which makes it very hard for policy changes to be made, even when in its own interests the Council has a pressing need to make them.

The emphasis on vague concepts of quality, standards and tradition is a product more of bureaucratic than party politics. The former secretary-general Sir Roy Shaw, who has a collectivist rather than conservative background, and who now is very much in opposition to the present Arts Council, wrote of an international conference he had attended:

> I found at Oslo that many of my fellow experts from Europe cared too little for what they sometimes disparagingly refer to as 'the heritage concept of culture'. I shall never forget having to fight single-handed to persuade a group of experts that it was essential to ensure the *quality* of the arts we foster. 'Quality', they unanimously assured me, was a purely subjective concept, far too vague to use in cultural policy. A few people in Britain say the same, advocating 'relevance' as an alternative to qualitative standards. If not resisted, such thinking could gradually subvert any cultural policy and produce a situation where 'anything goes'.[8]

Relevance smacks too much of the democratic influence which the Arts Council is constituted to exclude; 'anything goes' would mean a loss of control on the part of the cultural bureaucracy. Quality remains a numinous essence distilled from the judgements of the Council. Thus the 'arts' are defined as that which is done by professional artists, not the general activity of a whole culture. Although for political reasons *per capita* funding in Scotland is higher than in England, there is a marked metropolitan bias between London and the regions which makes 'provincial' only slightly less pejorative a term than 'amateur'. The policy of devolving money and clients to the twelve regional arts associations has not significantly altered this, and the effect of recent management changes has been to bind the regional arts associations more closely to the Arts Council in London.

The most important application of the arm's length principle has been that of the Arts Council towards its own policies. Until the 1980s, it was not the Council's policy to have one. The watchword was 'response', and the steady increase in government subsidy to the arts during the Sixties enabled it to contain any contradictions through expansion. (Though it is notable that after a brief flirtation with 'community arts' in the 1970s it has returned to the traditional academic structure which rigidly divides the various art forms.) From 1975 on, however, expansion has effectively ceased, and the Arts Council has been forced to reconsider its position.

The question of the Arts Council's function has become even more urgent since the election of a government committed to reducing public spending and rolling back the frontiers of the state. So far, we have been discussing the politics of patronage at a constitutional level. In party political terms, the Arts Council has been politicised not by the Left, as the arts establishment has always feared it might be, but by the Right.

In spite of traditional Conservative resistance to the idea of a Ministry of Culture, Norman St John Stevas, the first of Mrs Thatcher's arts ministers, made a positive move in that direction by separating the post from a junior ministry in the Department of Education and Science, and setting up the Office of Arts and Libraries. As Chancellor of the Duchy of Lancaster and Leader of the House, Mr Stevas qualified for a seat in the Cabinet, and thus the arts were politically represented at a higher level than at any time since Jennie Lee was first called Minister for the Arts in the Wilson government of the mid-1960s. Mr Stevas proposed to rationalise the government's spending on the arts, libraries and the heritage, and he began by warning arts bodies to look elsewhere for growth:

The arts world must come to terms with the situation and accept the fact that Government policy in general has decisively tilted away from the expansion of the public to the enlargement of the private sector. The Government fully intends to honour its pledge to maintain public support for the arts as a major feature of policy, but we look to the private sphere to meet any shortfall and to provide immediate means of increase. When the economy is restored to health we will no doubt be able to enjoy a higher level of public support than is possible at present.[9]

In 1980 the total arts budget for 1981/82 was cut by £10 million.

In spite of Mr Stevas's loyalty to government policy, his flamboyance, and sympathy for the social difficulties that government policy was creating did not endear him to Mrs Thatcher. In 1981 he was replaced by the relatively colourless Paul Channon, and the Arts Ministry returned to Education. Following the 1983 election Channon was replaced by Lord Gowrie, another colourful figure, who, as a published poet and a former art dealer, had the advantage of some knowledge and appreciation of the arts. The Office of Arts and Libraries became once more independent, but Lord Gowrie's other duty (beside running the Civil Service) was to act as a Treasury spokesman in the House of Lords. As part of the post-election government cuts in 1983, one of his first actions was to take back £1 million from the Arts Council's current grant, forcing it to go back on commitments to clients for the first time in its history. Lord Gowrie saw the arts through the abolition of the metropolitan county councils, before resigning in 1985 to become chairman of Sothebys' and Andrew Lloyd Webber's Really Useful Group. Under Lord Gowrie, subsidy for the arts had become a controversial issue, and it may be that his successor, Richard Luce, was chosen in order to dull the ardours Lord Gowrie had inspired.

Since it is they who appoint the membership of the Arts Council, all these ministers have been able to adjust its party political colouring. The selection process has been described by Kenneth Robinson: as chairman of the Arts Council he would 'suggest one or two names to the Minister, but equally he suggests names to me, and the appointment is a resolution of these different approaches.'[10] It is not publicly recorded whose approach needed most to be reconciled when in 1980 Alistair (now Lord) McAlpine, Treasurer of the Conservative Party and tenant of West Green, joined the Arts Council, in spite of his lack of belief in public subsidy for the arts. (McAlpine resigned from the Arts Council in 1981.)

There were more violent changes to the complexion of the Arts

Council in 1982, when Professor Richard Hoggart, a man of the Left, was effectively dismissed as Arts Council Vice-Chairman. 'No. 10 doesn't like him,' Robinson explained to the secretary-general, Sir Roy Shaw.[11] In 1982 both Robinson and Shaw's periods of office were coming to an end, which provided an ideal opportunity for these two key posts to change political hands.

Kenneth Robinson's replacement was Sir William Rees-Mogg, the former editor of *The Times*, and a convinced supporter of the government's monetarist economics. The Arts Minister, Paul Channon, said it 'was hardly surprising' to appoint 'somebody you respect and get on with and whose views on the arts you're more likely to be more in agreement with than not', thus confirming the political objectivity of the appointment.[12]

The choice of secretary-general was more controversial. Sir William selected a thirty-five year-old former Tory councillor in Bath, Luke Rittner, who had been running the Association for Business Sponsorship of the Arts. The concern was not Rittner's youth or inexperience, but the fact that the choice marked a shift of power in the Arts Council away from the secretary-general and to the chairman. When Sir Roy Shaw left the Arts Council in 1983 he attacked the complacency of the three previous arts ministers (including the last Labour minister, Lord Donaldson), and drew attention to the close link that now existed between the Council and 10, Downing Street. All the new appointments, he said, would qualify in Mrs Thatcher's phrase, as 'one of us', and he hoped that the Council was not becoming 'a creature of Government.'[13]

Since leaving office, Sir Roy Shaw has published his criticisms of the current Arts Council in *The Arts and the People*. He writes, 'There has been a decline in the power and influence of Council members themselves, which has meant an increase in the power not (as some journalists have suggested) of officers, but of the chairman.'[14] He gives us this insight into the deliberations of the Council:

> Membership of the Council was described as a privilege by Paul Channon and I believe some Council members felt the privilege so keenly that it seemed to them discourteous to argue with their chairman. Moreover, the issues before the Council were often so complex that many members could not grapple with them. I was not alone among officers in suspecting that papers they had carefully prepared were very often not read, or, if read, not understood.[15]

The issues that the Council had to deal with were indeed complex, but the primary question was how to deal with the changed political and economic climate of the Eighties. The end of steady growth in arts subsidy in 1975 had made the Council more, not less important, and it was forced to make the sort of artistic judgements that expansion had helped it to avoid. As a result, it became increasingly unpopular with the arts community that looked to it for support, even survival. In 1979 the Council was scrutinised by the Department of Education and Science, and by an internal enquiry conducted by the then vice-chairman, Jeremy Hutchinson. This enquiry revealed 'a widespread sense of malaise and a low level of morale' among the staff, while 'Council members, secretary-general, panel members and officers are all unclear as to the exact nature and extent of their authority and functions.'[16]

In December 1980 the Arts Council announced that it was cutting off the grants of no fewer than forty-one organisations. Cuts had never been seen on such a scale, and the announcements were handled badly, obviously causing considerable uproar from the unfortunate forty-one. The House of Commons Select Committee on the Arts in 1982 did not give the Arts Council a clean bill of health, again recommending that it should 'give more attention than it has shown in the past to long-term policy issues', and that the arts minister should review the way the Council was constituted – that is, how the membership of the Council was arrived at.[17]

The major threat to the Arts Council was the recommendation that the arts ministry should become a Ministry of Arts, Heritage and Tourism, with a minister of Cabinet rank with increased power and responsibilities that took in broadcasting and the cinema industry as well as tourism. A stronger ministry would mean a weaker Arts Council, which would lose some of its work to the regional arts associations and no longer be 'the sole channel of central government funding of the performing and creative arts'.[18]

As if to underline the point, in 1983 the covert system by which the arts minister had unofficially 'earmarked' funds for certain organisations, chiefly the national companies, within the overall Arts Council grant, became overt, when special funds were allocated by the Arts Minister to the Royal Opera House and the Royal Shakespeare Company. This was the result of a manoeuvre that had backfired on the government, when a management expert, Clive Priestley, had been appointed to investigate the financial working of the two companies. Both carried deficits and complained of underfunding, but it was assumed that this was due to their own extravagance. The Priestley Report found, on the contrary, that they were both efficiently run and indeed underfunded. Accordingly, the Arts Minister (now Lord Gowrie) set aside £2.8 million in the Council's 1984/85 grant-in-aid specifically for these institutions. At the same time he provided funds to write off the debts of other opera companies, so that a total of £4.1 million came with specific purposes from the Ministry. The arm's length principle was seriously eroded. By the end of 1983, however, Sir William Rees-Mogg had taken control of the Arts Council, and was preparing to defend the institution and the caste whose interests it represented against the very political forces that had put him there.

The abolition of the Greater London Council and the six other metropolitan councils – a Conservative commitment in the 1983 election – was not at first sight an issue which affected the arts, but it very rapidly became one. This top tier of local govenment, created by a Conservative reorganisation in 1972, covered the main urban regions of England, where most of the population is concentrated. The argument for abolition of the councils was that they were inefficient, and in a period when the government was doing all it could to reduce public spending, their budgets were insufficiently under control. There was also the simple fact that they were governed by Labour councillors. But because of their readiness to spend public money in the interests of social welfare, they were also significant supporters of the arts. As Sir William Rees-Mogg has commented: 'The arts represent less than one-hundredth of those councils' expenditure; an observer might well have supposed recently that the arts were their only function.'[19]

The pattern of local authority support for the arts has followed that of central government. Although there are examples of municipal initiative such as the foundation of the Bournemouth Symphony Orchestra in 1894, local arts subsidy did not become a legislative fact until the 1948 Local Government Act, which empowered – but did not impose a duty on – local authorities to support the arts up to the limit of a 6d rate. (There is no element in the government's central rate support grant allocated to the arts, as there is for museums and libraries.) As the 1982 House of Commons report on the arts put it: 'local authority support for the arts over the country as a whole is inadequate and can at best be described as patchy.'[20] Local authorities were estimated to spend only twelve per cent of their leisure and recreation budgets on the arts. The metropolitan county councils, however, were more mindful of the arts. Arts Council calculated that in 1984/85 the metropolitan county councils and the GLC spent £46 million on the arts, excluding film and museums.[21]

The government's answer to the problem that it was creating by abolishing the metropolitan councils was simple: just nine performing arts companies and five museums and galleries would be elevated to national status and directly funded by the Arts Council or the government. The rest of the arts organisations about to lose major funds would have to look to the smaller local authorities that inherited the defunct MCC's responsibilities, and to commercial sponsorship. This plainly would not do, and the threatened MCCs, especially the Greater London Council, used the fact of their importance to the arts (which included organisations such as the National Theatre) very skilfully in self-defence.

It was at this point that Sir William Rees-Mogg decided that the Arts Council would not simply have to respond to the situation that had been created, but that it would have to show itself capable of dealing with the crisis in such a way as to preserve itself as well as the threatened arts organisations. The result, after a long and intensive period of internal discussion and debate in the winter of 1983–84, was the document, *The Glory of the Garden*, published on 30 March 1984.

The Glory of the Garden – a quotation from Rudyard Kipling that betrays the gentry values behind the image of the arts as the floral embellishments to 'Our England' – is only obliquely concerned with the problems of the major metropolitan and industrial regions of the country. The focus lies in the subtitle 'A Strategy for a Decade', with its assumption that the Arts Council would still be in existence in 1994. The argument was that while London was, if not fully then adequately provided for, the regions were underfunded. Accordingly the Arts Council committed itself to a transfer of funds from the metropolis. It was apparently accepted that the overall funds available would not increase so as to be able to maintain London *and* the regions; the Council was therefore assenting to the monetarist argument that public spending had to be kept in check. As a result cuts would have to be made in the metropolis in order to achieve growth elsewhere. The original proposal was for the Arts Council to reduce its revenue (that is, annually funded) clients from 156 to ninety-four. In the increasingly sophisticated language of arts administration, cuts, savings and transfers would create a 'development programme' which, including a projected £1 million from future grant-in-aid, added up to £5.5 million.

When put in practice, this policy has meant, according to Sir William Rees-Mogg, 'a tiny shift, at most a three per cent shift, from metropolitan to regional art'.[22] But this was not the true object of the exercise. The purpose of *The Glory of the Garden* was to assert, in another of Mrs Thatcher's phrases, the Council's 'right to manage'. This was quickly assented to, both by an enthusiastic response from the Arts Minister, Lord Gowrie, who proceeded to earmark additional funds for the development strategy and, more importantly, agreed that the Arts Council would distribute the extra funds that would have to be made available if there was not to be complete chaos when the metropolitan councils disappeared. In April 1984, the month after *The Glory of the Garden* was published, Lord Gowrie announced that an extra £16 million would be made available to the Arts Council in order to meet the needs of arts organisations affected by abolition. The Arts Council argued that £37 million would be needed, and when the time came the element of 'replacement funding' in the Council's grant-in-aid for 1985/86 rose to £25 million. Although the concept of government funds for specific purposes had to be conceded, the Arts Council could argue that it had retained its position as the main distributor of the government's arts patronage.

Since we are still in a period of adjustment following the abolition of the GLC and the metropolitan county councils, it is right to record that when abolition took place in April 1986, there was not the collapse of arts organisations that was feared in 1983. The Arts Council was not able fully to replace the funds that were lost, but it and the government were able to persuade the more than sixty successor authorities to take up most of the responsibilities that they had inherited. The complete picture will not become clear until 1990, when the money earmarked by the government for replacement funding, which is intended to taper off, ceases altogether.

The main question, however, concerns the position of the Arts Council. Has it been rewarded for its efforts in extracting the government from the emotive tangle which it created by abolishing the metropolitan councils? Sir William Rees-Mogg has been rewarded, in that his chairmanship of the Council, due to end in 1987, has been extended for a further two years. The Arts Council has also retained its central position as a distributor of funds. But these funds have not been increased. The Arts Council's bid for grant-in-aid in 1986–87 was £161 million; it got £135.6 million, of which £25 million was replacement funding. Sir William said that he was naturally disappointed. More importantly, the arguments for a Ministry of Culture have grown stronger, so much so that in March 1987 the Council held an international conference entitled 'The Arts, Politics, Power and the Purse', in the hope of defending the arm's length principle. (This, it should be said, was the subtext, rather than the agenda, of the conference.) In the run-up to the 1987 general election all the opposition parties proposed strengthened arts ministries with a much wider sphere of control, and the reduction of the

Arts Council to an advisory position. While the opposition attempted to exploit the now accepted idea that there were votes in the arts, the Arts Minister, Mr Luce, was forced to acknowledge that 'the arts are more and more coming onto the political map.'[23] In the event, they do not seem to have got very far.

The Conservative party is committed to making no change – except in one significant area – in the current arrangements for the funding of the arts. The reason is that however much the Council may criticise the government in detail – and no agency or spending ministry is ever completely satisfied with its budget allocation – the Arts Council conforms best to its model for state patronage. Although the arm's length principle has been shortened to the length of a wrist, the government can continue to shield its policies behind the Council, while the Council willingly forecloses the possibility of democratic control over the distribution of public patronage, or any kind of debate over definitions. In his 1985 lecture Sir William, in a striking country house metaphor, compared the government to 'a good landowner [who] spends money looking after his tenants; he runs a good shoot and . . . looks after his family, and then each year he gives a £100 subscription to the local arts festival. One might call that man many things. One might regard him as an ornament of the House of Lords. But surely not a great patron of the arts.'[24] Yet however much the Arts Council may complain about the shortfall in funding, it has no option but to assent, like the humble tenant that it is, to the govenment's decisions – just as Council members and advisors have to assent to the decisions of the Arts Council.

Thus, although the Conservative government since 1979 has done more to politicise the management of the arts than any previous administration, and the arts have been recruited for purely economic purposes, they nonetheless retain a low priority as independent expressions of culture. Britain spends less on funding the arts than any other country in Western Europe. Total government spending on the arts in the United Kingdom allocated for 1987/88 is £339 million, less than a quarter of 1 per cent of the total government expenditure of £148 billion.

The administrative weakness of the arts is institutionalised. Responsibility for the whole cultural spectrum is dispersed over at least six different government departments: broadcasting is the responsibility of the Home Office, the film industry (but not the National Film School) the responsibility of Trade and Industry, buildings and ancient monuments are in the care of the Department of the Environment, which shares heritage issues with the Office of Arts and Libraries. The arts ministry has an establishment in 1987 of fewer than forty. In 1982 the House of Commons report complained of the department's response to the enquiry 'the document we received was slight and the oral evidence uneven' and concluded that it was 'incapable of having the impact we would like to see'.[25] It is no wonder then that the select committee 'gained the impression that the arts have reached an impasse'.

> The overwhelming weight of our evidence was that our arts organisations, including our great national companies and museums, are living on a knife-edge, in a chronic state of anxiety and frustration about the quality of their existence and even in some cases about their very survival.[26]

This condition, which affects the entire sphere of cultural activity, from the performing arts to education, has not changed. On his retirement as director of the National Gallery in December 1986, Sir Michael Levey told *The Times*: 'The present position is indefensible. It is deeply shocking that someone bears the title of Minister for the Arts and does nothing for them. It makes me wonder whether the arts would be better without a minister.' His anger took in the whole government. 'They don't understand what art is about. Very few have the courage to say "I am illiterate." Very few have the courage to say "Every time I see a book, I throw it on the fire." They're precious near to that in the visual arts, whose neglect has shown their basic lack of imagination.'[27]

The National Gallery is only one of the institutions which finds its purchase grant inadequate to compete on the international art market that has boomed, as more and more museums compete for major paintings. While the turnover at Sotheby's in the Autumn of 1986 was £331 million, and at Christie's £159 million, the Committee for the Review of the Export of Works of Art noted 'the continuing outflow of important objects and, in particular, of beautiful paintings, which, it seems, the nation cannot afford'.[28] In 1985/86 £10.7 million worth of what the Committee should have been able to prevent going abroad on 'heritage' grounds was exported because no British buyer could be found. The Museums and Galleries Commission would like to be able to double its grant to the Area Museums Councils by 1990. Museums which were founded on the principle of free access have had to introduce voluntary or compulsory charges, with a consequent reduction in the number of visitors.

The Ministry for the Arts has regularly claimed that government spending on the arts has increased 'in real terms'. In December 1985

Mr Luce told the House of Commons, 'In the past six years we have more than doubled the amount of money given to the arts. The Arts Council's funds have increased by seven per cent in real terms in the past six years.' But these figures are arrived at by applying a different system for calculating inflation. Instead of using the retail price index, which the 1982 report by Professor Alan Peacock, *Inflation in the Arts* confirms has the most application in the labour intensive cultural field, the government applies the Gross Domestic Product Deflator, which is used to calculate the cost of major capital items like warships. If the retail price index is applied, the Arts Council grant actually has fallen by 1.4 per cent. On this calculation, between 1979 and 1986 total government expenditure on the arts rose by 2.2 per cent, within which museums and galleries gained 8.5 per cent and the Arts Council, British Film Institute and the Crafts Council suffered a cut of 2 per cent. All figures for government expenditure are distorted by the provision of replacement funds to cover the abolition of the metropolitan councils, and the increasing demands on the budget of the Office of Arts and Libraries made by the construction costs of the new building for the British Library at St Pancras.[29]

Whatever claims are made on behalf of the government its policy remains that outlined by Mr Luce in September 1985. 'Let us be clear, there is no bottomless pit of public funds. This government is by no means alone in feeling the need to rein back expenditure in order to free resources for the private sector . . . The arts cannot therefore count on substantially more funds from central government. Nor do I think it would be healthy if they were able to do so.'[30]

Other ministries have applied the same monetarist logic to cultural expenditure. While the Arts Council has at best stood still, the British Council, which is funded by the Foreign Office and the Overseas Development Agency to promote Britain's cultural and technological skills abroad, has suffered a twenty-one per cent cut in real terms since 1979. The British Council's responsibility for cultural relations is a wide one, and the arts absorb only about seven per cent of the £86.6 million grant-in-aid for 1986/87. Much of the work is devoted to development projects for which it is contracted by government departments, including the teaching of English as a commercial language. But without the arts the Council's language laboratories would be teaching a language that has nothing to say.

At home, the government's attempts to bring down public spending have caused it to reduce its contribution to the rate support grants of local authorities, and take powers to impose limits on their budgets through rate-capping. This has inevitably made local authorities reduce their non-statutory spending on areas like the arts and cut back on their statutory responsibilities such as libraries. More than

200 public libraries have closed since 1979, and book funds have been cut by an average of thirty-five per cent at a time when the price of books has risen by sixty-seven per cent. The worst of the fall in the public provision for libraries took place between 1979 and 1984, when public libraries lost £5 million, school book funds £10 million, polytechnics and colleges £5.5. million, and university libraries £2.4 million. The Library and Information Services Council Report for 1986 (which describes such services as 'a national heritage') concludes of public libraries that 'the amount of money spent on books in real terms is about £5 million less at the end of the decade compared with the beginning, although bookstocks have increased by nearly seven per cent. More importantly, the proportion of expenditure allocated to books has fallen by nearly nine per cent during a period when book prices have increased at a rate significantly higher than the Retail Prices Index.'[31]

The Conservative government's emphasis on what it terms value for money has had a disturbing effect on education both at primary and secondary level where there have been shortages of books and materials, and a long-running industrial dispute with the teachers, and in the universities and polytechnics, where institutions have found themselves facing bankruptcy. By 1986 spending on universities had fallen by twenty per cent, there have been uneven staff cuts and posts left vacant, and 20,000 student places lost. But the effect has not been to increase efficiency, even in the engineering and technology departments the policy was supposed to favour, where it is reported that half of the posts are now difficult or impossible to fill. It was a sign of the times when, in 1985, the Convocation of Oxford University voted against awarding the Prime Minister an Honorary Degree. The editor of the *Times Higher Education Supplement* wrote:

> Today large parts of higher education have moved into permanent opposition, even internal exile. Mrs Thatcher's rejection at Oxford was not some fluke engineered by Balliol bolshies. This alienation of organised intelligence from the present government, and perhaps more generally from a state with apparently philistine values, will have serious consequences for the sensible conduct of public affairs well into the next century.[32]

Since then internal exile has become exile proper, as more and more senior academics leave for posts abroad. The drain of qualified scientists has spread to philosophers, art historians, historians, and professors of English. They are tempted abroad not only by higher salaries, but the knowledge that a higher valuation is being put on their work. Claude Rawson, an English Professor at Warwick University told the *Observer* why he was going to Yale: 'Inevitably my move has something to do with what is happening in British universities. I feel very disheartened about the prospect of spending the rest of my working life fighting for my work instead of doing it.'[33]

During 1986 the crisis provoked by the cutbacks in education led to a change of minister, and Sir Keith Joseph – who had begun his term of office by asking his officials what mechanism existed for closing down a university – was replaced by Kenneth Baker, who, with a general election in the offing, increasing spending plans at all levels. But this has not ended the sense of disaffection among the teaching profession, nor made up for the damage done since 1979. Yet it was a Conservative Minister for Higher Education, George Walden, who said, in December 1986: 'An intellectual culture is not a luxury, but a practical economic and political necessity.'[37]

It may be that an ill-educated and ill-informed public is precisely what the cultural policies of the 1980s have been intended to produce. An intellectual culture is also a critical culture, which is not prepared passively to accept the decisions made on its behalf by political appointees who are answerable to no one but themselves. But the economics of the arts are such that it is almost impossible for artists to survive without subsidy. The commercial sector is dominated by large conglomerates for whom the need to ensure a return on capital reduces risk-taking to a minimum, and whose critical calculations are based on the lowest common denominator, not the highest common factor. Public subsidy may sometimes be a minor budgetary element, but it is not only the financial contribution which allows a venture to break even: the granting of subsidy in itself becomes an important factor in gaining other forms of support. A grant from the Arts Council is a sign of approval from the official culture.

But although the Arts Council is charged with the nurture of contemporary culture, its structure is directed much more towards the conservation of traditional art forms than the evolution of new ones. Its emphasis is on the performing arts, which draw upon a defined tradition of past works, rather than on the creative arts which are engaged in the present day. Contemporary literature is hardly supported at all; contemporary art has been contained within a tradition of the avant-garde which has been shaped and defined by the Arts Council. Because it has acquired so many long-term clients, most of the Council's funds are already committed at the beginning of any one year. At most £1 million is available to develop new ideas and new works. It is true that the Arts Council does support new work in theatre, music, art and dance, but it has largely withdrawn from the support of individuals, indicating a loss of confidence in its ability to make creative choices. It prefers to support institutions, and work through existing clients rather than develop new ones. Project grants (small subsidies to individual endeavours by non-revenue clients) which offer the possibility of experiment and growth have been severely restricted by the need to maintain commitments to established revenue clients. Such new work as is presented is often restricted to the temporary enthusiasms of a rootless festival culture.

The established companies have been forced by economic necessity to restrict their experimental work in favour of commercially viable productions. Orchestras must limit their rehearsal time, and stick to a repeatable repertoire of a narrow range of conventional works. In all the art forms the number of performances and new productions has fallen, and the link between the subsidised and commercial sector has become much closer. Both the National Theatre and the Royal Shakespeare Company do more than take advantage of the transfer of productions to the West End, they programme their work with commercial transfers in mind, or, as in the case of the RSC with *Les Misérables*, begin with a commercial partnership. Under pressure to keep their auditoria full, the National revives plushly furnished pre-war farces, the RSC applies the production techniques developed by radical theatre groups in the late 1960s to plays from the classical repertoire – without the radicalism that inspired the originators to develop them. The progressive theatre of the Fringe is in decline, and the Royal Court, one of the few theatres still committed to new and politically engaged work, has to look to New York for support. Everywhere the scale of productions is reduced, outside the West End, where commercial theatre survives on expensive hollow spectacle.

The answer of both the government and the Arts Council to the gradual anaemia produced by the restriction of subsidy has been to encourage the growth of business sponsorship. When the Association for Business Sponsorship of the Arts was founded in 1976 some £600,000 a year was being spent by commercial enterprises on the arts. In 1986 commercial sponsorship was estimated to be between £25 and £30 million. (This sum excludes the philanthropy of John Paul Getty's gift of £50 million to the National Gallery, or the Sainsburys' gift of £25 million to build the National Gallery extension.) Government encouragement has been more than benign: in

1980 Norman St Stevas signalled the change of direction with a direct grant of £25,000 to ABSA. In 1984 Lord Gowrie launched the Business Sponsorship Incentive Scheme, administered by ABSA, under which new commercial sponsors have their sponsorship matched £1 for £1 by the government, up to a limit of £25,000, and established sponsors at a ratio of £1 to £3. In 1987/88 the Office of Arts and Libraries made available £1.75 million for matching grants.

Thus aside from the government money going directly to sponsor the sponsors, behind the appearance of free enterprise commercial sponsorship is still a form of government subsidy. As a form of advertising it is a charge allowable against the company's taxable income, and as with incentives like the new payroll giving scheme, it represents an element of government revenue forgone in the interests of a specific purpose. (In this respect, the main subsidy to the book publishing industry is zero-rating for VAT, although it is not certain how long this will continue.) But this is a form of subsidy without the 'disinterestedness' of the Arts Council. Commercial sponsorship is done not in the interests of the arts, but in the interests of the sponsor, most of whom wish to promote a product or a service, or more generally improve an image. As the secretary-general of the Arts Council, Luke Rittner has said: 'If prestige and the altering of a perception is what you're trying to do, then the arts can achieve that, and not necessarily very expensively.'[35]

Not surprisingly, industries which have a particular need to alter perception of themselves have found sponsorship very useful: the tobacco industry, which is restricted in other ways in promoting its products, has a long history of arts sponsorship. Peter Stuyvesant began its association with the London Symphony Orchestra in 1957, and promoted major art shows in the 1960s. Imperial Tobacco has given extensive support to the arts, including Glyndebourne Opera, which survives almost entirely on private benefactors and commercial sponsorship. Peter Taylor's *Smoke Ring: The Politics of Tobacco* quotes British Allied Tobacco's paid parliamentary consultant Sir Anthony Kershaw:

> It's an area which needs an awful amount of money, and it's an area where there are quite a lot of influential people who know leaders of the tobacco industry. Of course it's a prestigious thing to do amongst the select people of the country. I shouldn't think it makes very much difference to ordinary people, the fact that BAT sponsors an orchestra. I think it's very important that tobacco companies are not only seen to be, but actually are a caring sort of outfit which has got the interests of the nation at heart.[36]

Recently United Technologies Corporation, which has multiple interests, including two highly sensitive areas in Britain, cruise missiles and Sikorsky helicopters, has been sponsoring major exhibitions with the active support of the Arts Council. The art critic of the *Guardian*, Waldemar Januszczak has commented: 'It seems in such cases that cultural sponsorship is part of a softening up process, forming the vanguard of a larger economic strategy. Sponsors do not act out of corporate kindness or love of art but because cultural sponsorship is a relatively cheap and cost-effective form of advertising. By hitching themselves to the reputation of a great and quite essentially British artist, as UTC did when they sponsored the Stubbs exhibition at the Tate, the company basks in reflected glory.'[37]

The chairman of ABSA, Lord Goodman, has said, 'It is a splendid quality of business sponsorship that everywhere it recognises the integrity of the artist; and the principle of non-interference ranks high with those cultivated businesses which give the artist such vital support.'[38] But the arts organisations which are forced to devote increasing amounts of energy to the pursuit of sponsors are cynical about the principle of non-interference. United Technologies, for instance, warned a potential recipient of their sponsorship that they would have to undertake not to criticise any aspect of the Corporation's work – including the arms industry. Early in 1986 ABSA refused to award a matching grant under the Business Sponsorship Incentive Scheme to a production *The Resistable Rise of Arturo Ui* at the Crucible Theatre in Sheffield, which had been sponsored by the trades union NALGO. The reason for the refusal was that NALGO had mounted an exhibition in the foyer attacking the government's privatisation policies. The Arts Minister Mr Luce confirmed ABSA's decision, saying 'it would be quite unacceptable for taxpayers' money to be used to support party politics in this way.'[39]

The main point at which interference occurs, however, is the sponsor's choice of what, and what not, to sponsor. Inevitably new work, experimental work and any kind of art which challenges the cultural and economic *status quo* finds it almost impossible to secure sponsorship. The arts which do attract sponsorship are those which are the most prestigious, the most conventional and the most secure: the heritage arts. Any effort by the Arts Council to improve the imbalance in arts provision between London and the regions is countered by the weight of sponsorship in London. But even here the emphasis is on prestige events. Colin Tweedy, director of ABSA, has written: 'London highlights the concerns of the arts over sponsorship: while fifty per cent of the money spent in the United Kingdom goes to London, most of London's arts don't see a penny of it. It is the national companies and orchestras and the capital's galleries which

126

attract most sponsors and that have the time and resources to go out and find sponsorship.'[40]

Symphony orchestras and opera companies have been the most successful at raising sponsorship and donations. An analysis of awards under the Business Sponsorship Incentive Scheme showed that, although this was intended to encourage new sponsors and forms of sponsorship, music attracted 33.3 per cent, theatre 21.4 per cent, festivals 11.1 per cent, visual arts 8.5 per cent and opera 6 per cent. Community arts attracted 1.3 per cent, literature 2.1 per cent.

Commercial sponsorship can produce strange bedfellows: banks supporting the National Theatre production of Brecht's *Threepenny Opera*; the National Trust, its properties at times saturated with visitors, has its 1987 Handbook sponsored by the Ford Motor Company. The illustrations of Quinlan Terry's Richmond Riverside scheme in Clive Aslet's study are sponsored by the developers Haslemere Estates, who are discreetly boosted as 'sympathetic to a more humane architectural approach'.[41] As if to defend modern architecture against such sneers, forty-seven firms involved in the design, engineering and construction of new buildings contributed sponsorship to the Hayward Gallery exhibition *Le Corbusier: Architect of the Century*. The developers, Trafalgar House, were the principal sponsors, and twelve architectural firms and schools of architecture sponsored individual models of Le Corbusier projects, attaching their names to the designs of the great architect.

Commercial sponsorship is gradually altering the ecology of the arts, just as it has already changed the economics of sport. As Waldemar Januszczak has pointed out: 'In the long term the art world must surely learn to cut its coat to suit the available cloth. The rise in sponsorship has been paralleled by the rise in blockbuster exhibitions. These huge, expensive displays of artistic wealth do indeed cost a fortune to mount and advertise.'[42] The cultural shift that is taking place is being actively promoted by the Arts Council, which has employed a sponsorship officer since 1984. Critics at the Renoir exhibition in 1985 at the Arts Council's Hayward Gallery were handed instructions to acknowledge the show's sponsors, and similar pressures have been put on critics in other arm forms to mention the sponsors' names, even when their contribution is far smaller than the Art Council's.

The essential difference between Arts Council support and commercial sponsorship is that while the Arts Council is concerned with the development of an arts organisation and is committed to its long-term future, a commercial sponsor is not. It is merely exploiting an existing facility and has no obligation to continue its support. The object of commercial sponsorship is to provide a means for the sponsor to entertain its clients, its primary considerations are the

London factor, the Mozart factor, and the champagne tent. Few sponsorships last more than three years, and so a commercial patron can never replace the essential continuous subsidy needed for survival. A change of fashion, or a change in the profitability of a sponsor's company, can cause such patronage to disappear overnight. And as the director of ABSA Colin Tweedy has admitted, 'While business sponsorship is increasing, the majority of contributions are too small to have a significant effect on the financial needs of the UK arts.'[43]

Business sponsorship has already changed the language of the arts. Tweedy remarks that 'arts organisations often fail to understand that they are selling a product to a potential customer and have to deliver benefits accordingly.'[44] The Minister for the Arts speaks of 'the delivery of the art product' to 'consumers of art'.[45] This language has been enthusiastically embraced by the Arts Council, with such publications as *A Great British Success Story*, which presented its bid for increased government funding in 1986/87 in terms of a business prospectus: 'the money spent from the public purse on the arts is a first-rate investment, since it buys not only the cultural and educational elements, never more necessary at a time when work and leisure patterns are rapidly changing, but also a product with which we compete on equal or superior terms with the rest of the world. The arts are both at the heart of the tourist industry, and a major diplomatic and cultural aid.'[46] The term 'client', originally coined to describe the service relationship between the Arts Council and the arts organisations it was created to serve has reversed its meaning: now recipients of subsidy are the humble servants of the Arts Council.

The new emphasis is not on encouraging artists but marketing the arts, indeed, in marketing the Arts Council. In parallel with the development strategy of *The Glory of the Garden* the Council has put through an internal reorganisation that has reduced the influence of officers responsible for the individual art forms, and created a new marketing division, headed by a former account director at Saatchi and Saatchi. His appointment has made necessary four redundancies in the Arts Council's information library: information gives way to image. In December 1986 the Office of Arts and Libraries launched a new scheme to improve marketing the arts, with a budget of £250,000. The Arts Minister's plans to extend the principle of 'challenge funding' to the core grants of Arts Council clients, which emerged in the wake of the 1987 election, will narrow still further the opportunities for new work.

The arts are not seen to be the means by which a society engages in a critical dialogue to tease out the values by which it might live. They

128

are not even for enjoyment. They are for investment. The case is repeatedly made that the arts return more to the Exchequer by way of tax than they receive in subsidy, though as *The Times* commented: 'These arguments are uncomfortably reminiscent of the all-too-familiar proof that there is no such thing as an uneconomic coal mine.'[47] The economic arguments now being used in relation to the arts are not confined to Conservatives: the Labour party promised in the run-up to the 1987 general election that of the one million new jobs it planned to create, 40,000 would be in the arts.

A change in cultural perception has taken place which narrows the imagination and cramps the spirit. In the nineteenth-century museums were seen as sources of education and improvement, and were therefore free. Now they are treated as financial institutions that must pay their way, and therefore charge entrance fees. The arts are no longer appreciated as a source of inspiration, of ideas, images or values, they are part of the 'leisure business'. We are no longer lovers of art, but customers for a product. And as the marketing managers of the heritage industry get into full swing, the goods that we are being offered become more and more spurious, and the quality of life more and more debased.

VI

A FUTURE FOR THE PAST

On the top floor of the Wigan Pier Heritage Centre there is a small photographic exhibition. The pictures come from two sources: a series of Wigan people in the 1890s by a local Anglican clergyman, William Wickham, and a number of similar subjects taken in 1985 by a professional photographer, Kevin Cummins. Both sets of photographs have been enlarged to the scale of easel paintings, and are displayed on panels in such a way as to suggest at first glance that they are the same series. The introduction to the display makes this purpose clear: 'The intent of these two photographers was the same. To capture in the human face the individuality of society. Neither intended to prepare a comprehensive documentary but exercised their own eye for a picture. . . . Together they offer a distinctive, quirky, critical look at the way we were – the way we are.'[1]

The actual photographs tell a different story. Those by William Wickham were taken with the anthropological eye of a Victorian clergyman: his images were used as lantern slides for lectures. Because of the length of exposure required, his subjects, a postman, workmen, people in the street, have had time to compose themselves for the camera, and accept, rather than participate in, its presence. The texture of the exhibition prints, whose scale is far beyond the facilities that would have been available to Wickham, is pleasing because of a slight deterioration in their surface, and the effect of their transfer from glass negatives to modern printing paper. We cannot be sure that the compositions are precisely as Wickham intended: the prints have been bled off the paper and appear to have been cropped. One image, of unusual animation, shows children on a canal barge; it seems certain that this is an accidental detail enlarged and reframed from a bigger subject.

In the photographs by Kevin Cummins both the photographer and the people he photographed have become entirely self-conscious. His miners and Orwellian old men actively collaborate in the quick performance of a modern single-reflex camera; they instinctively understand the dramatic framing and cropping of contemporary advertising. By using fast film and high contrast printing, Cummins produces effects that are deliberately nostalgic and picturesque, as though he were trying to match the interesting textures of Victorian photographs, but with a different tonal range.

The result is entirely post-modernist: a re-working of an inherited vision, but with all the self-consciousness of the intervention of the medium. Unlike the clergyman's prints, Cummins's 35-millimetre negatives have been printed up so as to leave a border of white between the edge of the image and the sides of the paper it is printed on. The subject is not the scene caught in the camera's view-finder, but the entire negative, with sprocket holes and frame numbers adding their own signs of self-awareness. Its edges are not crisp, but chancy and indeterminate, floating off into the surrounding whiteness. The slightly rounded corners echo the format of abstract paintings by Rothko, which have just the same floating relationship between fields of colour and the straight edge of the canvas. The effect on the photographs is to flatten them into thin skins; their exploration of texture turns out to be a micro-millimetre deep.

'The way we were – the way we are' offers us a modernised past, and an antiqued present. A contemporary photographer can only confront his subject through quotation of the past; his own aesthetic is drawn from the technology of his medium, which actually serves to disengage him from the image he presents. That is why these images are post-modernist.

Post-modernism is a difficult concept, because it is composed of contradictory elements. As the art historian Clive Dilnot has said, 'What is the "post-modern"? It is first, an uncertainty, an insecurity, a doubt.'[2] The prefix suggests that it is whatever is happening to contemporary culture, now that the great wave of modernism, lasting roughly from Picasso's first cubist paintings to the dropping of the atomic bomb, is over. Post-modernism is modernism with the optimism taken out. The prefix also suggests that nothing has happened since. At worst, post-modernism is the complete rejection of the present that leads to King's Walden Bury and the lifestyle of the New Georgians. At best, radical post-modernists recognise that we are living in a broken culture, and must make the fragments into a new pattern, not shore them up against our ruin.

Though contradictory, both attitudes betray an unhealthy dependence on the past. The uncertainty of the present has produced, in Clive Dilnot's words, a 'post-modern culture – "retro" in everything from films to fashion, the cult of pastiche and parody, the over-estimation of style, the tacky scenography of architectural post-modernism as exemplified in the buildings of Michael Graves or Terry Farrell, the new appeal to the "cult-of-the-master" and "traditional painterly values" of the neo-expressionist painters – [which] appear as all too easily understood signals, from a modernist perspective at least, of a cultural decline.'[3] But there is a distinction to be made between the reactionary post-modernism of Quinlan Terry (who would reject the term altogether), and the pastiche and parody in much contemporary art.

Part of the reason for late twentieth-century doubt and uncertainty is that our mutual relations across the planet have become instantaneous, a vast computer network, but almost entirely abstract. If, metaphorically, Renaissance society was organised around the heirarchy of single-point perspective, and nineteenth-century society shaped by the division of labour that developed from the railway line to the assembly line, then the model for the society of the fourth machine age is the microchip: an abstract pattern printed on a flat surface that functions in series, accumulatively, but unlike a classical façade or a steam engine, has no emblematic or visual power.

Imaginatively deprived in the present, we turn to images of the past, either in reactionary revivalism, or in a spirit of ironic quotation that emphasises the distance between the source and its recycled imagery. While the microchip is assembled in binary series, the post-modernist format is the collage, an assembly of fragments without ruling pattern or perspective. Narrative is deliberately broken or disrupted, special relations are subjected to chance, and a self-referring consciousness of medium is all. Without perspective it becomes an art of surface, of appearance, not content. Waldemar Januszczak has described the curious – and literally superficial – similarities between the abstract metal sculpture of Richard Serra and the neo-expressionist paintings of Anselm Kiefer, shown together in 1986 at the Saatchis' new gallery:

> The texture of poverty used to be called 'patina'. It is the appearance of old age, a kind of spurious spirituality endowed upon the art work by the passage of time. Serra's giant sculptures may be grand new pieces acquired by the Saatchi Museum this year but they look as if they have survived countless wet winters rusting in the docks.[4]

Kiefer, meanwhile, 'works the picture surface as a farmer works a field.' But while the aggressive scale and workmanship of such pieces may be attractive to an art patron who is one of the foremost practitioners of mass communication, even their monumentality is a monument to failure:

> Patina is that warm, worn, safe, familiar feeling worshipped by immature, materialist societies shell-shocked from

progress. Post-modern collectors buy new art covered in patina for the same reason as post-modern architects build Neo-Georgian buildings, to gain a respite from the decision making processes of the present. They are literally buying second-hand time.[5]

Just as Kiefer's surfaces are built up by encrusting the paint with sand and straw, and incorporating bits of agricultural machinery, or Julian Schnabel thickens his textures with broken china, modern architects construct their buildings on the principle of collage. The wall caption introducing James Stirling's designs for the extension to the Staatsgalerie in Stuttgart, on exhibition at the Royal Academy, officially sanctions its description as

> a collage of architectural fragments. The plan is a comment on Karl Friedrich Schinkel's Altes Museum in Berlin of 1824, the north wing borrows from the Swedish neo-classical style of the 1930s, while the offices at the rear of the building copy Corbusier's house design at the Weissenhof Siedlung built in Stuttgart in 1927, and the air ducts look as though they have been borrowed from the Centre Pompidou.[6]

The use of quotation develops into the art of pastiche, as the line between revivalism and re-use becomes thinner and thinner. Fredric Jameson, who argues that the binding abstract pattern of the modern world is the computerised network of multi-national capitalism, has pointed out the crucial difference between the critical art of parody, and the derivative art of pastiche:

> Pastiche is, like parody, the imitation of a peculiar mask, speech in a dead language: but it is a neutral practice of such mimicry, without any of parody's ulterior motives, amputated of the satiric impulse, devoid of laughter and of any conviction that alongside the abnormal tongue you have momentarilly borrowed, some healthy linguistic normality still exists. Pastiche is thus blank parody.[7]

The best that much contemporary art can do is revel in its authenticity, it is an art of the polaroid, the photocopier, the screen-print, where the only creativity is chance. The emotional equivalent of pastiche is nostalgia, which deliberately falsifies authentic memory into an enhanced version of itself. It is a strangely powerless emotion, a sweet sadness conditioned by the knowledge that the object of recall cannot – indeed, must not – be recovered.

The self-consciousness of contemporary art has produced, as Jameson notes, 'the waning of affect'.[8] With the exhaustion of modernism we no longer experience the excitement of new discoveries, and must therefore seek out the shock of the neo. But as Jameson points out, even the most exaggerated gestures of contemporary artists and performers 'no longer scandalise anyone and are not only received with the greatest complacency but have themselves become institutionalised and are at one with the official culture of Western society.'[9] Absorbed into the system that, with the potential satisfaction of most material wants has now turned to the production of immaterial commodities such as 'style', art has lost its revolutionary vigour.

Increasingly, real experiences are overtaken by pseudo-events. In his *Sociology of Nostalgia* Fred Davis points out the increase of nostalgia, not for a personal past, but for the media events of the music and popular press of the period. The process is reinforced by the media's appetite for consuming itself: real events are filtered by the media, and then recycled. As television swallows its own tail with repeats and revivals, the time lapse between the event and its nostalgic reprise becomes shorter and shorter.

Television, with its continuity and ubiquity, is the ultimate emblem of the post-modernist screen. Degraded electronic images are projected onto the inside of a glass tube, upon whose surface we may tap, but whose images we cannot touch. The flatness, the depthlessness, the superficiality of contemporary culture is expressed by these networked pictures with their constantly shifting collage of images and points of view. Drama and real life become so indistinguishable that every summer weekend the inhabitants of Washburn Valley in Yorkshire are plagued with sightseers seeking the mirage of Emmerdale Farm.

Post-modernism and the heritage industry are linked, in that they both conspire to create a shallow screen that intervenes between our present lives, and our history. We have no understanding of history in depth, but instead are offered a contemporary creation, more costume drama and re-enactment than critical discourse. We are, as Jameson writes, 'condemned to seek History by way of our own pop images and simulacra of that history, which itself remains for ever out of reach'.[10]

The past may be beyond recovery, but it is highly susceptible to recuperation. As Professor Peter Fowler has warned: 'The past is not an absolute quantity but a relative set of values. Such indeed would seem to be the case if we look at the acceptable pasts portrayed in European literature and art over the last 200 years.'[11] History as an academic discipline is not dead, though its practitioners seem to prefer the detailed surfaces of specialised topics to seeking out the deep structures of longer periods of time. In Ireland, where history is still murderously fought over, the pamphlets published by the Field Day Theatre Company represent a contemporary attempt to relate the past to the present in a critical and creative way.[12]

In Britain the popular approach to history is to rewrite it. This has served its purpose, obscuring the military disasters of 1940 with 'the Dunkirk spirit'. The recovery, indeed recuperation, of the wreck of the Mary Rose, is a specific example: Henry VIII's battleship went down as a result of pure incompetence; its recovery – which also very nearly went wrong – is presented as a technological triumph. Patrick Wright has identified the resonances the recovery of the Mary Rose struck during the Falklands War.[13] Only some deep royal memory may have caused Prince Charles, who was present to watch the raising of the ship that Henry VIII had watched go down, to decline to step onto the wreck once it had broken the surface, on the grounds that he was wearing the wrong kind of shoes.

At times history is not so much recovered, as recruited. In the Spring of 1987 British Nuclear Fuels, desperate to prove the harmlessness of the Windscale Nuclear Power Station (which in order to confuse memories of an earlier accident had been renamed Sellafield) sought to attract visitors to the site by laying on train trips drawn by the Flying Scotsman. 'You get hauled into the nuclear age by that most famous engine of the steam age' wooed the advertising copy, revealing an unconscious awareness of people's reluctance to be hauled from one age to another. Steam is now safely part of the industrial heritage, let nuclear power adopt the same camouflage.[14]

Imperceptibly, history is absorbed into heritage. But a heritage without a clear definition, floating on the larger frame of the present. The first annual report of the National Heritage Memorial Fund, for 1980–81 confronted the absence of any definition in the Act of Parliament that had set it up, and concluded that the question of definition was unanswerable:

> We could no more define the national heritage than we could
> define, say, beauty or art. Clearly, certain works of art
> created by people born in this country were part of the
> national heritage – paintings by Turner and Constable, for
> instance, or sculptures by Henry Moore or Barbara
> Hepworth – as were buildings such as Chatsworth or
> Edinburgh Castle. But, beyond that, there was less
> assurance. So we decided to let the national heritage define
> itself. We awaited requests for assistance from those who

believed they had a part of the national heritage worth saving. . . .

The national heritage of this country is remarkably broad and rich. It is simultaneously a representation of the development of aesthetic expression and a testimony to the role played by the nation in world history. The national heritage also includes the natural riches of Britain – the great scenic areas, the fauna and flora – which could so easily be lost by thoughtless development. Its potential for enjoyment must be maintained, its educational value for succeeding generations must be enriched and its economic value in attracting tourists to this country must be appreciated and developed. But this national heritage is constantly under threat.[15]

The thought process is revealing: a refusal to define the heritage is followed by a definition that embraces art, buildings and landscape, and then justifies its existence as an economic resource. But the key to the passage is that the heritage is something that is *under threat*. The threat is multiple: there is decay, the great fear of a nation that feels itself in decline; there is development, the great fear of a nation that cannot cope with change; there is foreign depredation, the great fear of a nation that is losing works of art it acquired from other nations in the past to economically more powerful nations like the United States and Japan.

And so we polish up a history that has been reselected and rewritten. The past is made more vivid than the present. It never rains in a heritage magazine. By the use of microchip technology the past is made more engrossing with slide presentations, taped sounds, film and ghost rides to the tenth century. The past becomes more homogeneous than the present, it becomes simply 'yesteryear'; if there is development it is 'progress' where continuity is discovered in the place of chance, and where rooms and houses are restored to a uniform conception of a period, and objects are standardised by their display. Alternatively, all styles and periods are represented as equally valid, to the extent that even the stylistic confusion of Wigan's Officers' Club achieves its own 'period style'. The past is domesticated and, by regulation, made safe; it is rescued, removed, rebuilt, restored and rearranged. As David Lowenthal has pointed out:

History thus transformed becomes larger than life, merging intention with performance, ideal with actuality. Acting out a fantasy our own time denies us, we remake the past into an epoch much like the present – except that we have no responsibility for it. The present cannot be moulded to such desires, for we share it with others; the past is malleable

137

because its inhabitants are no longer here to contest our manipulations.[15]

The distance between this polished past and actuality can have a paradoxical effect, as a former director of the Ironbridge Gorge museum admits:

> One of the changes I see of the new wave industrial museum is that it creates a sort of curious nostalgic, rose-coloured picture of a sort of Pickwickian industrial past which bears no relation to reality, but which we like to imagine. And we do like to doctor our history to suit our image picture, don't we? A lot of what is presented isn't based on scholarship at all but upon attitude and emotion. So I think the anti-industrial attitude is an antipathy towards industry now, but we're quite happy to look at history of say fifty years ago, because its part of our heritage.[17]

It may be that the ultimate pastime of the 1980s is to visit the forges and farmyards of open air museums in order to watch other people work.

Yet we have no real use for this spurious past, any more than nostalgia has any use as a creative emotion. At best we turn it into a commodity, and following the changed language of the arts, justify its exploitation as a touristic resource. The result is a devaluation of significance, an impoverishment of meaning. Yet to admit that the commodity on sale is fraudulent would be deeply unsettling, especially to the salesmen. David Lowenthal writes

> To recognise that the past has been altered understandably arouses anxiety. A past seen as open to manipulation not only undermines supposed historical verities but implies a fragile present and portends a shaky future. When we know that hoary documents are regularly forged, old paintings imitated, relics contrived, ancient buildings modernised and new ones antiquated, the identity of everything around us becomes dubious. When a past we depend on for heritage and continuity turns out to be a complex of original and altered remains enlarged by subsequent thoughts and deeds, if not an outright sham, we lose faith in our own perceptions.[18]

Had we more faith in ourselves, and were more sure of our values, we would have less need to rely on the images and monuments of the past. We would also find that, far from being useless except as a diversion from the present, the past is indeed a cultural resource, that the ideas and values of the past – as in the Renaissance – can be the inspiration for fresh creation. But because we have abandoned our critical faculty for understanding the past, and have turned history into heritage, we no longer know what to do with it, except obsessively preserve it. The more dead the past becomes, the more we wish to enshrine its relics.

Disconnected, it seems, from the living line of history by world war, and the successive strokes of modernisation and economic recession, we have begun to construct a past that, far from being a defence against the future, is a set of imprisoning walls upon which we project a superficial image of a false past, simultaneously turning our backs on the reality of history, and incapable of moving forward because of the absorbing fantasy before us.

This is the meaning of the heritage industry, though it still means 'whatever you want' to those who call it to their aid. The subtext of the museum shop filled with heritage reproductions, which is of growing economic importance to the museum economy, is that it is now possible to buy the past off the shelf. Stephen Bayley, the director of the Conran Foundation's new museum of design at Butler's Wharf, in London's docklands, has remarked: 'In a sense, the old nineteenth-century museum was somewhat like a shop, you know, a place where you go and look at values and ideas, and I think shopping really is becoming one of the great cultural experiences of the late twentieth century . . . The two things are merging. So you have museums becoming more commercial, shops becoming more intelligent and more cultural.'[19] Thus Ralph Lauren decorates his New York store with the trappings of an English country house; Paul Smith scours the country for the abandoned shelving of gentlemen's outfitters, in order to make his modern store like a tailored museum.

At times the conservation movement appears to exclude even those with deep roots in the soil that is to be protected. Lady Sylvia Sayer has described the operations of the Dartmoor Preservation Trust, founded, as it happens, by her great-grandfather and grandfather:

> A farming member suggested that the Association should try to recruit more working class people, 'not people who read the posh newspapers but the ones who read the *Daily Mirror*, because there are more of them.' But a massive local membership is likely to mean the entry of elements that favour unrestricted motoring and caravanning and resent restraints on building or advertising in the National Park.

> Many local councillors and native Dartmoor inhabitants
> whose forbears had to fight the moor to wring a living from it
> are likely to support anything that tames the wilderness, such
> as more roads, quarries or reservoirs or any other
> development promising further employment or economic
> advantage. Dartmoor is unique and of national importance,
> and can no more be left in the care of local farmers than
> Oxford's colleges can be left in the care of the car workers of
> Cowley.[20]

The farmers of Dartmoor and the car-workers of Cowley are similarly excluded from a say in the definition of what constitutes the arts that are worthy of subsidy and encouragement. One wonders what the black inhabitants of Bristol's St Paul's area will make of the Museum of the Empire projected for the city.

The social programme of the heritage industry is a return to a Georgian England where an agreeable pastoral and small country town life is somehow fenced off from the deprivation, squalor and crime of the major inner cities and now semi-derelict industrial areas. The suggestion of the Home Secretary, Douglas Hurd, that the crime statistics of the ten worst inner-city areas should be separated out, because they are 'distorting' the crime statistics is not only a manipulation to match the regular downwards recalculation of the unemployment figures, but also an attempt psychologically to isolate the mob back into the criminal 'rookeries' which once supplied the compulsory colonists of Australia.[21] The final irony is that many of the inhabitants of the inner cities are the descendants of voluntary immigrants to this country.

The arts, meanwhile, are to be a sedative to the mob. Richard Luce is pleased as Minister for the Arts that:

> They serve particularly as a counterpoint to the darker side
> of recent social changes: the increase in destructiveness,
> hooliganism and violence. I have been struck on recent visits
> to Liverpool and Glasgow by the important role the arts,
> even on a humble level, can play in giving youngsters from
> the most disadvantaged backgrounds a new interest in life
> and in rebuilding their confidence.[22]

The sedation encouraged by the official arts that have become incorporated into the closed culture of the heritage has produced a massive, long-term inertia in cultural and economic life which is as much the cause as the consequence of the climate of decline. As Neal Ascherson has argued: 'It is commonly and comfortingly said that there is nothing wrong with British institutions – "the finest in the world" – but that they are not working well at present because the economy is in such a bad state. The reverse is true. The reason the economy does not work is that British institutions are in terminal decay.'[23] The heritage, as the success of the cult of the country house demonstrates, is part of the cultural system of defence these institutions deploy.

The heritage industry presents a history that stifles, but above all, a history that is *over*. The development of Britain has reached a finite state that must be preserved at all costs against the threat of change. Any shift away from that finite state must be interpreted as decline. Patrick Wright has argued that the National Trust lacks the capability:

> To think positively of history as transformation,
> discontinuity or change. The National Trust arrives at its
> superior definition of the nation through a purifying cult of
> permanence, continuity and endurance. The nation is not
> seen as a heterogeneous society that makes its own history as
> it moves forward, however chaotically, in the future. Instead,
> it is portrayed as an *already achieved* and timeless historical
> identity which demands only appropriate reverence and
> protection in the present.[24]

As we loll back on a close-clipped bank in the garden of some National Trust property on a drowsy summer Sunday, it is not difficult to be persuaded that the tangible past is desirable and attractive. The feeling lingers with us, even as we struggle to get out of the car park. All this, the garden, the house, the weather, must be preserved for ever. But the conservation movement brings other ideas besides a certain concept of national identity in its train. It introduces the idea that our own time has nothing to contribute to the achieved culture of the past. The heritage, far from compensating for present discontents, either as a spiritual or crudely economic resource, quietly increases them, by holding before us the contrast between a decaying present and an ever improving and more appealing past. The true product of the heritage industry is not identity and security, but entropy. If history is over, then there is nothing to be done.

It has been argued that the process by which the energy of the nation will be reduced to the ultimate state of inert uniformity has been going on for a long time. M. J. Wiener, in *English Culture and the Decline of the Industrial Spirit*, traces the loss of entrepreneurial energy to the mid-nineteenth century – just that period when the conservation movement began to get under way – when the aggressive, industrial values of the rising bourgeoisie began to be tempered by the conservative, pastoral values of the aristocracy, and the concept of service promoted by the growing, and also middle-class, bureaucracy. The process was an elaborate trade-off between industry and aristocracy that enabled the latter to retain its privileges: 'Power was peacefully yielded in return for time and for the acceptance of many aristocratic values by the new members of the élite.'[25] The exchange – or rather transmutation – of 'power' into 'values' has maintained the monarchy intact, and built new country houses as well as preserved old ones. But the price has been a fatal loss of dynamism, the drive for expansion and productivity has given way to care for prestige.

The economic crisis of the 1970s, Wiener argues, 'was preceded by a century of psychological and intellectual de-industrialisation.'[26] The 'greening' of the 1970s was in part a response to the thrust of modernisation of the 1960s. But as Sidney Pollard warned in *The Wasting of the British Economy* (1983) 'The rustic idyll may have its attractions, but it could only be enjoyed by a maximum of around ten million. The British population of fifty-five million cannot exist without urban concentrations and factories, and these have to be efficient.'[27] The true nature of our industrial decline has been masked by the exploitation of North Sea oil, which has been used as a screen to cover the loss of international trade in manufactured goods. This too has been a means of avoiding change, not carrying it through.

This is a cultural, as much as a political issue. As Michael Heseltine has argued, 'We cannot expect services to sustain the country's economy without the manufacturing base to sustain them, especially since the value added by manufacturing is three times that added by services.'[28] The former Secretary of State for the Environment, paradoxically the instigator of the creation of English Heritage, is well aware that 'for the past twenty-five years we in Britain have lived off our past and have moved too slowly to improve our performance.'[29] Both managements and trades unions have lost the dynamism either to respond to the so-called 'liberation' of Thatcherism, or the calls for revolution of the Left. The trades unions have become victims of their own traditions just as much as the industries which made their creation necessary.

The last time that there was any sense of national mobilisation was during the Falklands War, which proved to be the encapsulating heritage event: a battle for a distinctly 'British' and utterly remote piece of moorland, long neglected by the industrial corporation that owned it, against a group of fascist foreigners out of a Bulldog Drummond story. The campaign was short, though not without risks which recalled earlier foreign expeditions, from Henry V to the BEF in 1940. The conduct of the campaign was skilfully managed – at least in the media – so that the final outcome appeared to be an extended version of the Royal Tournament, though with the added drama of actual loss of life. The effect of the Falklands expedition was to strengthen Britain's inward conservatism. 'We' had won. The position of the Falklands remains unchanged.

Yet if 'we' are to come to terms with the inevitable disruptions of change, then we must seek to understand it, and not reject it as only more evidence of decline. The continuity between past and present must be maintained, the difficulty is that it is far harder to rethink the way we treat the past, than to make the present conform to the image of the past that we have created. There is no denying that the erasures of modernisation and recession have been an enormous disruption, but if we are to make any sense of them, they must be confronted, however painfully. It is no solution to retreat into a fake history: we need to recover the true continuity between past and present by coming to terms with previous failures. If the disruptions they have caused are so great that it seems impossible to make sense of them then we must make new meanings, not retrieve old ones.

The impulse of conservatism is to ignore events which do not match our understanding or expectation, to isolate innovation, and to label anything that does not fit into established patterns as deviation. Disenchantment with the present drives us back into the past, or such elements of the past as survive into the present day, and their protection becomes the sole object of our energies. Fortunately even museum directors will acknowledge that the past was not the static entity that the heritage industry makes it appear to be. The present director of the Ironbridge Gorge Museum, Stuart Smith, warns

> If you are not careful you will wallow in nostalgia, in this sort of myth that the past was wonderful. I personally believe the past was awful. And that sustains me all the time because I believe what is going to come in the future is much better. And museums have a vital role, I feel, to play in telling people that the past did produce some wonderful things, did produce great people, but their main contribution to society was actually changing society, and I still believe that we can change society, that people who come to my museum can actually look at what other people have done in the past, and go away and do similar things themselves.[30]

If, as seems likely, Britain is moving into a 'post-industrial' age, then the commodities of culture and information will be expected to stand in more and more for manufactured goods. Yet we are preparing for this revolution very badly, by closing off the currents of culture, and reducing our educational output in all spheres. It seems ironic that a Conservative Minister for Higher Education, George Walden should write:

> If Conservatives want change within continuity, and to enrich the present with a knowledge of the past, we would do well to encourage a little more familiarity with it. A country losing touch with its own history is like an old man losing his glasses, a distressing sight, at once vulnerable, unsure, and easily disoriented.[31]

As the distinguished art historian E. H. Gombrich has said of the threat to the arts and humanities caused by the cuts in higher education, 'An informed and critical attitude is the only viable antidote we have against the danger that has threatened and continues to threaten the rational outlook of whole generations who are intoxicated by bogus history.'[32]

Heritage, for all its seductive delights, is bogus history. It has enclosed the late twentieth century in a bell jar into which no ideas can enter, and, just as crucially, from which none can escape. The answer is not to empty the museums and sell up the National Trust, but to develop a critical culture which engages in a dialogue between past and present. We must rid ourselves of the idea that the present has nothing to contribute to the achievements of the past, rather, we must accept its best elements, and improve on them. It will be necessary to distinguish carefully between the ideas of a single closed tradition appropriated by the Right and the genuine tradition that involves a continual renewal of the best ideas and values of a society from one generation to another. The definition of those values must not be left to a minority who are able through their access to the otherwise exclusive institutions of culture to articulate the only acceptable meanings of past and present. It must be a collaborative process shared by an open community which accepts both conflict and change.

The elements of such a critical culture already exist, in the ideas and activities of contemporary artists who have continued to struggle with the material of the present, in spite of their increasing neglect by the institutions of culture which have been the subject of this book. The heritage industry is not interested in art as a process of making and renewal, but in works of art that are already achieved, where they can be absorbed as symbols of the general culture the heritage institutions support. Culture is the work of a whole society, but art is made by individuals, and it is to such individuals that we must look for fresh perceptions of the present and new approaches to the legacy of the past.

Artists criticise the product of culture every day and in a very practical way, by taking them and refashioning them into something new. Films like Hanif Kureishi's *My Beautiful Laundrette*, Denis Potter's work for television, plays like Jim Cartwright's *Road*, novels like Martin Amis's *Money*, the installations of David Mach and Tony Cragg, the performances of Michael Clark, all testify to a violence, but also a vigour that the insecurity of cultural conservatism makes it anxious to exclude. These are not mere works of social realism that derive their power to affront by presenting a particularly grim contemporary reality: they have a richness of language and texture and suggest mutations of form that can alter our perception of the material world and release its potential. Nor are contemporary artists incapable of making creative and critical use of the past, as Peter Ackroyd's novel *Hawksmoor* or Nigel Williams's play *Country Dancing* show.

One of the first conditions for the emergence of a critical culture, then, is to disconnect the function of the artist as creator, from the function of the artist as wealth-creator, or simply job-creator. With the enthusiastic collaboration of the arts bureaucracies that depend on subsidy-distribution for their salaries, politicians of all hues defend public funding of the arts on grounds that have nothing to do with what artists have to say, and everything to do with the turnover they can achieve. As already argued, this has changed the language of the arts, and in such a language there are things it becomes impossible to say.

This is not an argument against subsidising the arts. One of the many ironies of the present situation is that a philistine government has done as much to stimulate the growth of a heritage industry by starving museums of funds, as by encouraging business sponsorship. This *is* an argument for freeing the artist to return to his or her true function, which is to find expressions for the images, ideas and values by which the rest of us may live.

If the first condition of a critical culture is to return artists to their vocation, the second is to accept that their imaginations must be free to look at the present rather than the past. In reality, the present is a more exciting and risky place than the comforting simulacrum of a triumphant, undivided nation that the heritage industry tries to carry forward from the past into the present. If we abandon ourselves to the rapt contemplation of the past, the demoralisation of artists who necessarily can only work in the present, will be complete.

The third, and subsequent conditions for a critical culture are the responsibility of artists themselves: to penetrate the screen of the past and unmask the present; to rediscover their creative energies and attack the material of today in order to re-shape the future. And if a critical culture is to begin anywhere, it must begin by criticising the heritage industry, before we drown in honey and aspic.

It may be argued that the technocratic society of the fourth machine age is incapable of creating the transcendent values that would bind the creatively conflicting elements of an open society together, and that the only reservoir of values is the past. Yet the very drive towards the production of goods which contribute to the new industries based on the technology of information is an opportunity to recover and enlarge the creative possibilities of culture. Instead of the miasma of nostalgia we need the fierce spirit of renewal; we must substitute a critical for a closed culture, we need history, not heritage. We must live in the future tense, and not the past pluperfect.

Notes

Notes

Chapter I

1. George Orwell, *The Road to Wigan Pier* (first published 1937), Penguin, 1962 p.19; p.160.
2. ibid., pp. 15–16.
3. Introduction by Peter Lewis to *The Way We Were*, by Alastair Gillies, Wigan Pier Publications, (n.d.), p.1.
4. Eric Steed, *Wigan Pier, A Canal Trail*, Wigan Pier Publictions, (n.d.), p.13.
5. John Brown, John Brown Marketing and Development Services, typescript report, March, 1983.
6. loc. cit.
7. Promotional leaflet for The Officers' Club, Barrack Street, Wallgate, Wigan.
8. The Museums Association, *Museums UK: The Findings of the Museums Data-Base Project*, compiled by David Prince and Bernadette Higgins-McLoughlin, 1987.
9. Interview with the author for 'A Future for the Past', BBC Radio 4, 1986.
10. House of Commons, *Historic Buildings and Ancient Monuments*, First Report of the Environment Committee, Session 1986–87, HMSO, 1987. This and *English Heritage Monitor, 1986*, BTA/ETB Research Services, 1986, are the sources for the statistical information that follows.

11. John Myerscough, *Facts About the Arts 2*, Policy Studies Institute, 1986, Chart 15.1, p.292.
12. *The Road to Wigan Pier*, op.cit., pp. 104–5.
13. Peter Conrad, 'Don't Look Back', *Tatler*, April, 1986.
14. ibid.
15. Godfrey Smith, *The English Season*, Pavilion, 1987, p.8.
16. Adrian Woodhouse, 'Dishing up the loot at Broadlands', *London Daily News*, 24 February, 1987.
17. Alvilde Lees-Milne and Derry Moore, *The Englishman's Room*, Viking, 1987; Felicity Wigan, *The English Dog at Home*, Chatto, 1986.
18. Sarah Mower, 'Retro Mania', *Guardian*, 8 January, 1987.
19. Edith Holden, *The Country Diary of an Edwardian Lady*, Michael Joseph, 1977.
20. Press Release by Angex Ltd., 'The 1986 Ideal Home Exhibition', February, 1986.
21. *Environmental Interpretation*, March, 1987, p.6.
22. quoted in Robert Hewison, 'Museums are one of our few growth industries', *Listener*, 26 June, 1986.
23. Patrick Cormack, *Heritage in Danger*, New English Library, 1976, p.11–12.
24. quoted in Robert Hewison, 'Museums . . .', op.cit.

Chapter II

1. Ian Nairn, 'Outrage', *Architectural Review* (June, 1955), Vol. 117, No. 2, p. lxxi.
2. Lionel Brett, *Landscape in Distress*, The Architectural Press, 1965.
3. quoted in Martin Pawley, 'Johnson's journey into space', *Guardian*, 1 December, 1986.
4. quoted in Michael Heseltine, *Where There's A Will*, Hutchinson, 1987, p.195.
5. Colin Amery and Dan Cruickshank, *The Rape of Britain*, Paul Elek, 1975, p.10, and see Christopher Booker and Candida Lycett Green, *Goodbye London*, Collins/Fontana, 1973.
6. quoted in Peter Marris, *Loss and Change*, Routledge, 1974, p.43.
7. British Tourist Authority, *Britain's Historic Buildings: A Policy for their Future Use*, BTA, 1980, p.19.
8. Marion Shoard, *The Theft of the Countryside*, Temple Smith, 1980, p.99.
9. loc. cit.
10. *Britain's Historic Buildings*, op.cit., p.25.
11. Daniel Bell, *The Coming of Post-Industrial Society* (first published 1973), Penguin, 1976, p.42.
12. Christie Davies, *Permissive Britain: Social Change in the Sixties and Seventies*, Pitman, 1975, p.2; p.201.

13. Alan Sked, *Britain's Decline: Problems and Perspectives*, Blackwell, 1987, p.28.
14. Department of the Environment, *Transforming our Waste Land: The Way Forward*, HMSO, 1986, p.14.
15. Michael Heseltine, op.cit., pp. 142–3.
16. 'Prince attacks "prison" factory', *Independent*, 6 May, 1987.
17. Tamara Hareven and Randolph Langenbach, in *Our Past Before Us: Why Do We Save It?*, ed. David Lowenthal and Marcus Binney, Temple Smith, 1981, p.115.
18. loc. cit.
19. Interview with the author, 'A Future for the Past', BBC Radio 4, 1986.
20. Fred Davis, *Yearning for Yesterday: A Sociology of Nostalgia*, Macmillan, 1979, p.105.
21. ibid., p.105.
22. Michael Wood, 'Nostalgia or Never: You Can't Go Home Again', *New Society*, 7 November, 1974.
23. Roy Strong, introduction to Patrick Cormack, *Heritage in Danger* (second edition), Quartet, 1978, p.10.

Chapter III
1. Evelyn Waugh, *Brideshead Revisited* (first published, 1945, revised 1960), Penguin, 1962, p.7; p.331.
2. *The Treasure Houses of Britain: 500 Years of Private Patronage and Art Collecting*, ed. G. Jackson-Stops, Yale University Press, 1985, p.11.
3. ibid., p.10.
4. 'Cultural Diplomacy: Britain's Washington coup', *The Economist*, 2 November, 1985.
5. Clive Aslet and Alan Powers, *The National Trust Book of the English House*, Viking/National Trust, 1985, p.8.
6. Roy Strong, *The Destruction of the Country House 1875–1975*, Thames & Hudson, 1974, p.7.
7. quoted in Montagu of Beaulieu, *The Gilt and the Gingerbread: or How to Live in a Stately Home and Make Money*, Michael Joseph, 1967, p.89.
8. *Treasure Houses*, op.cit., p.27.
9. James Lees-Milne, *Caves of Ice* (first published 1983), Faber, 1984, p.94.
10. ibid., p.172.
11. quoted in *Britain's Historic Buildings*, op.cit., p.10.
12. Nigel Dennis, *Cards of Identity*, Weidenfeld, 1955, p.119.
13. Noel Annan, 'The Intellectual Aristocracy', *Studies in English Social History*, ed. J. H. Plumb, Longman 1955, p.285.
14. Evelyn Waugh, op.cit., p.8.
15. Robin Fedden, *The Continuing Purpose: A History of the National Trust, its Aims and Work*, Longman, 1968, p.70.
16. Clive Chatters and Rick Minter, 'Nature Conservation and the National Trust', *Ecos: A Review of Conservation*, Vol. 7, No. 4 (Autumn, 1986), pp. 25–32.
17. Anne Spackman, 'National Trust accused of nature neglect', *Independent*, 6 December, 1986.
18. *The Times*, 9 August, 1974.
19. Patrick Cormack, *Heritage in Danger*, New English Library, 1976, p.6; (second edition) Quartet, 1978, p.8.
20. Memorandum of the National Trust to the Select Committee on a Wealth Tax, House of Commons 696, Vol. II, 384, HMSO, November, 1975.
21. Roy Strong, *Destruction. . . .*, op.cit., p.7–10.
22. *Heritage in Danger* (1976), op.cit., p.35.
23. ibid., p.100.
24. quoted in Arthur Jones, *Britain's Heritage: The Creation of the National Heritage Memorial Fund*, Weidenfeld, 1985, p.63.
25. quoted in *Britain's Heritage*, op.cit., p.192.
26. ibid., p.120.
27. National Trust, *Annual Report*, 1985, p.4
28. ibid., p.6.
29. *Continuing Purpose*, op.cit., p.129.
30. John Cornforth 'John Fowler', *National Trust Studies 1979*, ed. G. Jackson-Stops, Sotheby Parke Bernet, 1978, p.40.
31. Andrew Dickson, 'National Trust Youth Theatre', *Environmental Interpretation*, March, 1987, p.17.
32. National Trust, *Annual Report*, 1986, p.4.
33. *Treasure Houses*, op.cit., p.76.
34. quoted in *Heritage in Danger*, 1976, op.cit., p.39.
35. Clive Aslet, *The Last Country Houses*, Yale University Press, 1982.
36. J. Martin Robinson, *The Latest Country Houses*, Bodley Head, 1984, p.7.
37. ibid., p.28.
38. ibid., p.29.
39. ibid., p.26.
40. Clive Aslet, *Quinlan Terry: The Revival of Architecture*, Viking, 1986, pp. 184–5.
41. Roger Scruton, 'The Architecture of Leninism', *The Aesthetic Understanding:*

Essays in the Philosophy of Art and Culture, Carcanet, 1983.
42. *Quinlan Terry*, op.cit., p.155.
43. ibid., p.83.
44. ibid., p.108.
45. 'Open the door to your own royal retreat in the heart of Sussex', Wimpey's promotional leaflet for Brantridge, 1987.
46. Peter York, *Modern Times*, Futura, 1984, p.22.
47. Alexandra Artley and J. Martin Robinson, *The New Georgian Handbook*, Ebury Press, 1985, p.46. (italics theirs).
48. Laura Ashley, *Laura Ashley Home Decoration 1985*, Laura Ashley Ltd., 1985.
49. Polly Devlin, 'Paradise Lost', *Country Living*, January, 1987.
50. *Quinlan Terry*, op.cit., p.121.

Chapter IV
1. Office of Arts and Libraries, press release OAL/70, 27 November, 1986.
2. *Museums UK*, op.cit., p.23.
3. *English Heritage Monitor*, 1977, BTA/ETB Research Services, 1977, p.16; p.18.
4. Interview with the author, 'A Future for the Past', BBC Radio 4, 1986.
5. R. A. Buchanan, *Industrial Archeology in Britain*, Penguin, 1972, p.19.
6. *The Economist*, 24 May, 1969.
7. *Industrial Archeology in Britain*, op.cit., p.20.
8. Anthony Burton, *Remains of a Revolution*, Andre Deutsch, 1975, p.8.
9. *Museums UK*, op.cit., p.59.
10. Peter Dunn 'Cowboys who would save the Rhondda', *Independent*, 31 January, 1987.

11. P. A. Faulkner, 'A Philosophy for the Preservation of our Historic Heritage', *Journal of the Royal Society of Arts*, Vol.126 (1978), p.457.
12. loc. cit.
13. ibid., p.471.
14. P. J. Fowler, *Our Past Before Us*, op.cit., p.61.
15. Max Hanna and Marcus Binney, *Preserve and Prosper: The Wider Economic Benefits of Conserving Historic Buildings*, SAVE Britain's Heritage, 1983, p.31.
16. *Historic Buildings and Ancient Monuments*, op.cit., p. xxxix.
17. *Preserve and Prosper*, op.cit., p.31.
18. Michael Heseltine, *Where There's A Will*, op.cit., p.164.
19. ibid., p.158.
20. quoted in *Industrial Archeologists' Guide 1969*, ed. Neil Cossons & Kenneth Hudson, David & Charles, 1969, p.73.
21. Montagu of Beaulieu, *The Gilt and the Gingerbread*, op.cit.
22. English Heritage, promotional leaflet.
23. *Historic Buildings and Ancient Monuments*, op.cit., p.xv.
24. *Museums UK*, op.cit., p.104.
25. Interview with the author, 'A Future for the Past', BBC Radio 4, 1986.

Chapter V
1. William Rees–Mogg 'The Political Economy of Art', Arts Council, 1985, pp.3–4. (A subtitle 'An Arts Council Lecture' gives this the status of a official policy document.)
2. ibid., p.4
3. House of Commons, *Public and Private funding of the Arts*, HMSO, 1982, p.

4. ibid., p.3.
5. ibid., p.2.
6. Lord Goodman, 'The Case against arts cuts', *Observer*, 25 March, 1984.
7. House of Commons, *Public and Private Funding of the Arts*, HMSO, 1982, Q800.
8. quoted in Nicholas Pearson, *The State and the Visual Arts*, Open University Press, 1982, p.99.
9. quoted in Harold Baldry, *The Case for the Arts*, Secker & Warburg, 1981, p.34.
10. *Public and Private Funding of the Arts*, op.cit., Q803.
11. Roy Shaw, *The Arts and the People*, Jonathan Cape, 1987, p.44.
12. quoted in Sandy Craig and Carole Woddis, 'How the Arts Council keeps it in the family', *City Limits*, 18/24 February, 1983.
13. Jeremy Jehu, 'Shaw hits out at "complacency" of arts ministers', *Stage*, 7 July, 1983.
14. *The Arts and the People*, op.cit., p.48.
15. ibid., p.49.
16. quoted in Janet Watts, 'Patronage behind closed doors', *Observer*, 2 March, 1980.
17. *Public and Private Funding of the Arts*, op.cit., p.xlvii.
18. ibid., p.xlvi.
19. The Arts Council, *The Glory of the Garden*, 1984, p.vii.
20. *Public and Private Funding of the Arts*, op.cit., p.xciii.
21. Arts Council press release, 6 June, 1985.
22. 'The Political Economy of Art', op.cit., p.7.
23. Comment made during a debate held by the National Campaign for the Arts at the National Film Theatre, 29 April, 1987.

24. 'The Political Economy of Art', op.cit., p.3.
25. *Public and Private Funding of the Arts*, op.cit, p.xxxviii; p. xxxvii.
26. op.cit., p.xxvi; p.lxxi.
27. Nicholas Shakespeare, 'Time to grant a growing-up', *The Times*, 31 December, 1986.
28. *Export of Works of Art 1985–86*, HMSO, 1986, p.1.
29. This paragraph uses the arguments and calculations deployed by Simon Crine in 'Has Government Spending on the Arts Increased?', National Campaign for the Arts *News*, Spring, 1986.
30. Speech to ASTMS conference, 17 September, 1985.
31. House of Commons, *Report by the Minister for the Arts on Library and Information Matters during 1986*, HMSO, 1986, p.11.
32. Peter Scott, 'Keeping the dons disaffected', *The Times*, 22 May, 1985.
33. Judith Judd, 'Eng. Lit. professors join brain-drain', *Observer*, 14 December, 1986.
34. George Walden, 'The many-layered illusions of our cultural decomposition', *The Times*, 20 December, 1986.
35. quoted in Peter Taylor, *Smoke-Ring: The Politics of Tobacco*, p.124.
36. ibid., p.117.
37. Waldemar Januszczak, 'No way to treat a thorough-bred', *Guardian*, 15 February, 1986.
38. Lord Goodman, *ABSA Annual Report*, 1985/86.
39. Elizabeth Swift, 'Tory poodle jibe for sponsor group', *Stage*, 20 February, 1986.
40. Colin Tweedy, 'Sponsor-ship in Partnership', *Greater London Arts Quarterly*, Spring, 1987, p.22.

41. *Quinlan Terry*, op.cit., p.193.
42. 'No way to treat a thor-oughbred', *Guardian*, op.cit.
43. Colin Tweedy, 'The Eco-nomics of Arts Sponsorship in the United Kingdom', *Cultural Policy* (Council of Europe), No. 1–2/86.
44. loc. cit.
45. Richard Luce, 'Frame-work of Opportunity', National Campaign for the Arts, *News*, Autumn, 1986.
46. Arts Council, *A Great British Success Story*, 1985, p.11.
47. *The Times*, 6 March, 1985.

Chapter VI
1. Wall caption, 'The Way We Were', Wigan Pier Heritage Centre.
2. Clive Dilnot, 'What is the Post-Modern?', *Art History*, Vol. 7, No. 2 (June, 1986), p.245.
3. loc. cit.
4. Waldemar Januszczak, 'Shine of Steel', *Guardian*, 17 September, 1986.
5. loc. cit.
6. Wall caption, 'Towards A New Architecture', Royal Academy, 1986.
7. Fredric Jameson, 'Post-Modernism, or the Cultural Logic of Late Capitalism', *New Left Review*, No. 146 (July/August, 1984), p.65.
8. ibid., p.60
9. ibid., p.56
10. ibid., p.71.
11. P. J. Fowler, *Our Past Before Us*, op.cit., p.65.
12. *Field Day Pamphlets, 1–12*, Field Day Theatre Com-pany, Derry, 1983–86.
13. Patrick Wright, *On Living in an Old Country*, Verso, 1985, pp. 162–191.
14. Advertisement in the *Guardian*, 13 April, 1987.

15. quoted in Arthur Jones, *Britain's Heritage*, op.cit., pp.206–7.
16. David Lowenthal, *The Past is a Foreign Country*, Cambridge University Press, 1985, p.356.
17. Interview with the author, 'A Future for the Past', BBC Radio 4, 1986.
18. *The Past is a Foreign Coun-try*, op.cit., p.411.
19. Interview with the author, 'A Future for the Past', BBC Radio 4, 1986.
20. Lady Sylvia Sayer, *Our Past Before Us*, op.cit., p.139.
21. 'Tories to take rise out of crime', *Guardian*, 6 April, 1987. For the social reality of Georgian England see Robert Hughes, *The Fatal Shore*, Col-lins Harvill, 1987.
22. Press release, Office of Arts and Libraries, OAL/16, 11 March, 1986.
23. Neal Ascherson, 'Ancient Britons and the Republican Dream', *Political Quarterly*, Vol.57, No. 3 (1986), p.300.
24. Patrick Wright, 'Mis-guided Tours', *New Socialist*, July/August, 1986, p.34.
25. M. J. Wiener, *English Cul-ture and the Decline of the Industrial Spirit*, Cambridge University Press, 1981, p.12.
26. ibid., p.157.
27. quoted in Alan Sked, *Brit-ain's Decline*, op.cit., p.39.
28. Michael Heseltine, *Where There's A Will*, op.cit., p.90.
29. ibid., p.88.
30. Interview with the author, 'The Man Who Made Beam-ish', BBC TV, 1986.
31. George Walden, *The Times*, 20 December, 1986, op.cit.
32. E. H. Gombrich, 'The embattled humanities', *Uni-versities Quarterly*, Vol. 39, No. 3 (Summer, 1985), p.196.

Index